# EVERYDAY BAKES TO SHOWSTOPPER CAKES

MICH TURNER MBE

# EVERYDAY BAKES TO SHOWSTOPPER CAKES

Take your creations from simple to
stunning in a few easy steps

Photography by Lisa Linder

FRANCES
LINCOLN

# INTRODUCTION

*Welcome all bakers – beginner, seasoned, professional, amateur, occasional or prolific! In this book I have curated a collection of delicious recipes that can be baked and enjoyed every day or as an indulgent treat.*

Imagine you have an extra special occasion, a celebratory event or social party that warrants something more – ramping up your cake from an everyday bake to a showstopper cake. Much like taking your wardrobe from day to night, this book aims to maximise each recipe by showing you skilfully, and rather cleverly, how to accessorise your everyday bake into a showstopper cake!

Over the past 20 years with Little Venice Cake Company I have had the privilege of creating in excess of 20,000 bespoke cakes. My philosophy has always been to combine totally indulgent cakes with intricate hand-craftsmanship to showcase an unrivalled portfolio of completely bespoke, refined opulent creations.

With this book I have focused on delicious recipes with mouthwatering flavours and ingredients such as chocolate, mango, passion fruit, salted caramel, peanut brittle, popcorn, ginger and lemon. Even the simplest cakes have been carefully balanced to maximise flavour and texture with a variety of options and skills to suit every day – from traybakes to tiered cakes, cupcakes to piñata cakes, and loaf cakes to layer cakes.

To turn each of these bakes into a showstopper I have included more advanced hand-finishing elements to challenge your craft skills – helping you combine inspiration and creativity to produce something fun, luxurious and guaranteed to impress. These recipes are designed as a launching pad for many of your own ideas. The only limit is your own imagination and each one can be turned into something truly unique.

I wanted to include a variety of cakes to suit the occasion and recipient – from baby shower and christening cakes through to early years birthdays with my Pirate and Unicorn Piñata Cakes (see pages 154–161) to the fun Pigs and Sheep (see page 34). From Valentine's to Mother's Day, Easter to Halloween there are projects to take you right though the year, with a bounty of seasonal Christmas treats and bakes, too.

Like many of my books, I have endeavoured to develop your skills and to inspire you to further explore your own innovation and creativity. You will find top tips, hints and alternative suggestions throughout the book.

Whether you are baking for family or friends, to celebrate or make amends, there's an occasion for every special cake – whether it's an Everyday Bake or a Showstopper Cake!

Thank you for investing in this book – I hope it brings you as much joy as I have had creating it.

# CUPCAKES

# CHOCOLATE CHIP CUPCAKES

*'Oh hello lovely chocolate chip cupcake!' These beauties are the perfect everyday indulgence – satisfyingly smooth, moist chocolate cupcakes with velvety chocolate chips. I've finished them with a simple chocolate glace icing and chocolate shavings. Contrasting paper cases add a touch of super sophistication.*

**Makes 16 cupcakes**

*For the cupcakes*
125g (4oz) plain flour
100g (3½oz) golden caster sugar
100g (3½oz) soft brown sugar
35g (1¼oz) cocoa powder
1 tsp bicarbonate of soda
½ tsp baking powder
1 tsp salt
120ml (4fl oz) buttermilk
80ml (3fl oz) sunflower oil
1 large egg
1 tsp vanilla extract
1 shot espresso topped up to 120ml
    (4fl oz) with boiling water (or
    1 heaped tsp coffee granules
    made with boiling water)
70g (3oz) dark chocolate chips

*For the icing*
150g (5oz) icing sugar
1 tbsp cocoa powder
freshly boiled water

*For the decoration*
chocolate shavings (use a vegetable
    peeler along the edge of a bar of dark
chocolate to make chocolate shavings)

## TO MAKE THE CUPCAKES

1   Preheat the oven to 170°C fan (190°C/375°F/Gas 5) and place 16 cupcake cases in a cupcake tin.
2   Sift all the dry ingredients apart from the chocolate chips together in a large bowl.
3   In a separate bowl, combine the buttermilk, sunflower oil, egg, vanilla extract and coffee.
4   Stir the wet ingredients into the dry ingredients using a hand balloon whisk and mix to a smooth batter.
5   Transfer the batter to a jug and pour the batter into each cupcake case until two-thirds full (about 45g/1½oz).
6   Sprinkle the chocolate chips on the surface of each cupcake – these will bake into the cakes in the oven.
7   Bake for 20-25 minutes until risen and set.
8   Remove from the oven and leave to cool in the tins for 5 minutes before transferring to a wire rack to cool.

## TO MAKE THE ICING

1   Sift together the icing sugar and cocoa powder. Add freshly boiled water a teaspoon at a time until you have a thick chocolate icing.

## TO ASSEMBLE THE CAKES

1   Spoon a little icing on top of each cooled cupcake and finish with a sprinkle of chocolate shavings.

The cupcakes are best eaten on the day they are made – but will keep in a cake tin at room temperature for up to 3 days. Suitable for freezing – freeze in a suitable container with a lid. Defrost at room temperature.

# CHOCOLATE CHIP, PEANUT BUTTER AND SALTED CARAMEL CUPCAKES

*Fully loaded, bursting with chocolate, smothered in peanut buttercream, packed with salted peanut brittle – these are the ultimate showstopper when it comes to indulgent chocolate chip cupcakes. The flavours, textures, sights and sounds satisfy on every level – and although they are more time consuming to make – you will reap the rewards – and make many new friends!*

**Makes 16 cupcakes**

1 quantity of Chocolate Chip Cupcakes (see page 12)

*For the peanut butter frosting*
175g (6oz) unsalted butter, softened
125g (4oz) smooth peanut butter
250g (9oz) icing sugar

*For the peanut brittle*
150g (5oz) salted roasted peanuts
200g (7oz) caster sugar

*For the chocolate ganache*
150g (5oz) unsalted butter, cubed
300g (11oz) dark chocolate (70% cocoa solids), broken into pieces
75ml (3fl oz) double cream

*For the decoration*
chocolate shavings (use a vegetable peeler along the edge of a bar of dark chocolate to make chocolate shavings)

**TO MAKE THE PEANUT BUTTER FROSTING**

1   Beat the ingredients together to make a smooth peanut buttercream.

**TO MAKE THE PEANUT BRITTLE**

1   Spread the peanuts out on a large sheet of non-stick baking paper on a baking tray.

2   Heat the sugar over a medium–high heat in a heavy, non-stick frying pan until it has completely melted and coloured to a rich golden amber colour. Do not stir the caramel – simply swirl the pan. Remove from the heat and pour the caramel over the peanuts to create interesting shapes.

3   Leave to set and then break the brittle into shards.

4   Store any remaining brittle in a sealed container in the fridge for up to 4 weeks.

**TO MAKE THE CHOCOLATE GANACHE**

1   Place the butter and chocolate in a large bowl and melt, either over a pan of simmering water or in the microwave, until the butter has melted and the chocolate has softened.

2   Bring the cream to a rolling boil in a small saucepan and pour over the chocolate and butter. Stir with a rubber spatula until fully combined, smooth, rich and dark.

3   Set aside 4-6 tablespoons of the ganache for the cupcakes. Store the remaining ganache in a container with a lid, either chilled for up to 4 weeks or in the freezer for 3 months.

$\longrightarrow$

CUPCAKES

## TO ASSEMBLE THE CAKES

1  Spoon the buttercream into a large piping bag fitted with a star nozzle. Starting in the middle of the cupcake, pipe swirls of buttercream to the outer edge and then up to a flourish. Continue until all the cupcakes are frosted.

2  Warm 4–6 tablespoons of the ganache in a bowl over simmering water or in the microwave until smooth and flowing (but not runny). Transfer to a small piping bag. Snip off the end with scissors and drizzle the ganache over the cupcakes.

3  Decorate each cupcake with a shard of peanut brittle and dust with the chocolate shavings. Now stand back, and admire your work – a round of applause please! You're welcome!

These cakes are best eaten on the day they are made – but will keep in a cake tin at room temperature for up to 3 days. Suitable for freezing - freeze in a suitable container with a lid. Defrost at room temperature.

# EASY MARBLE CUPCAKES

*Marble cake combines the best of both worlds and our two most preferred flavours – creamy vanilla cake and indulgent chocolate sponge. The secret is to have both batters the same consistency. The contrasting colours and flavours are always a delight when you bite into these fresh baked wholesome and hearty cupcakes. Serve warm from the oven, pure and unadulterated.*

**Makes 18 cupcakes**

*For the cupcakes*

150g (5oz) unsalted butter

150g (5oz) golden caster sugar

3 large eggs, beaten (weigh the eggs to ensure you have the same weight as the butter and sugar: 150g/5oz)

2 tsp vanilla bean paste

135g (4¼oz) self-raising flour

30–50ml (1–2fl oz) milk

1 tbsp cocoa powder

## TO MAKE THE CUPCAKES

1   Preheat the oven to 170°C fan (190°C/375°F/Gas 5) and place 18 cupcake cases in cupcake tins.

2   Cream the butter and sugar together in a large bowl until pale and fluffy.

3   Add the beaten eggs slowly until fully incorporated.

4   Divide the mixture between 2 bowls. Stir the vanilla bean paste into one of the bowls and then fold in 75g (3oz) of the flour – add milk as necessary to achieve a dropping consistency.

5   To the other bowl, add the remaining flour and the cocoa sifted together. Add milk as necessary to achieve a dropping consistency.

6   Transfer the vanilla and chocolate cake batters to separate large piping bags and snip off the ends with scissors (or use teaspoons to fill the cases).

7   Deposit both the vanilla and chocolate cake batters in each cupcake case until just over half full. Swirl with a cocktail stick to achieve a marbling effect.

8   Bake for 20-25 minutes until golden and baked evenly.

9   Leave to cool in the tin for 5 minutes before lifting out onto a wire rack to cool.

These are best eaten on the day they are made – but will keep in a cake tin at room temperature for up to 2 days.

## TOP TIP

Allow time for the batter to cream fully before adding the eggs – this will ensure your cakes are light and even when baked. Ensure eggs are at room temperature and added slowly (this will prevent curdling and ensure the cakes bake evenly).

# MARBLE PUP-CAKES

*Calling all dog-lovers! These cute Pup-cakes are fun to make with the family and guaranteed to brighten your doggie days! Make these 'pup-tastic' cakes to celebrate National Dog Day, a children's party or bake sale. I love the slight nuances in these canine creatures' characters – the cheekier the better. You wont be able to resist naming them!*

**Makes 18 Pup-cakes**

1 quantity of Easy Marble Cupcakes (see page 19)

*For the buttercream*
200g (7oz) unsalted butter
400g (14oz) golden icing sugar, plus extra for dusting

*For the chocolate ganache*
150g (5oz) unsalted butter
300g (11oz) dark chocolate (70% cocoa solids), broken into pieces
75ml (3½fl oz) double cream

*For the decoration*
40g (1½oz) fondant sugar paste per cupcake – you will need a combination of vanilla, chocolate and a blend of both colours
Royal Icing (see page 199), mixed with black food colouring

## TO MAKE THE BUTTERCREAM

1 Beat together the butter and icing sugar in a large bowl until light and fluffy.

## TO MAKE THE CHOCOLATE GANACHE

1 Place the butter and chocolate in a large heatproof bowl and microwave on medium for 1–2 minutes to gently soften.

2 Meanwhile, bring the double cream to a rolling boil in a small saucepan. Remove from the heat and pour over the chocolate and butter. Stir with a rubber spatula until the ganache is fully melted, smooth and glossy.

3 Leave to cool before stirring 5 tablespoons into the buttercream.

Store any leftover ganache in an airtight container in the fridge for up to 14 days or in the freezer for up to 3 months. Return to room temperature or gently melt in the microwave before using.

→

CUPCAKES

**TO ASSEMBLE THE CAKES**

1   Use a small cranked palette knife to spread chocolate buttercream onto the cupcakes. Hold the palette knife at an angle to shape and smooth the buttercream to a nice rounded mound. Refrigerate for 10-15 minutes to firm.

2   Colour the fondant sugar paste into shades of dark brown, tan and ivory.

3   Knead the dark brown sugar paste until soft and pliable but not sticky and roll out to a thickness of 2-3mm (⅛ inch) on a work surface lightly dusted with icing sugar. Stamp out 7cm (2¾-inch) circles with a round cutter.

4   Moisten the back of one of the fondant discs with a little cooled, boiled water and press and smooth into shape over the buttercreamed cupcake.

5   Repeat until you have all the bases covered in various shades of fondant sugar paste.

6   For the muzzle, choose a contrasting-colour fondant sugar paste and this time, stamp out 5cm (2-inch) round discs. Moisten and fix each one into position towards the base of each cupcake – to allow space for the eyes and ears.

7   Roll the dark brown fondant sugar paste into small jelly-bean -shape noses and fix in position with a little water.

8   For the ears, roll out the dark brown fondant sugar paste slightly thicker (3mm/⅛ inch) and use a 3cm (1¼-inch) cutter that has been pinched to create an elongated shape to stamp out shapes for the ears. Shape and mould each ear and place on a work board lightly dusted with icing sugar to firm.

9   To finish, fit a piping bag with a No 1.5 nozzle and fill with the black royal icing. Pipe the eyes and mouth on each Pup-cake, changing their facial expression slightly as you go.

10  Turn each pair of ears over and pipe a line of black royal icing along the outer edge of each ear. Turn over and press the pairs of ears simultaneously and firmly into position on each cake to ensure they are applied evenly and symmetrically. Allow the Pup-cakes to dry and firm for 1 hour.

Store in an airtight container at room temperature and eat within 3 days. Not suitable for freezing once decorated.

# MARBLE RING CAKE WITH DOUBLE CHOCOLATE DRIP

*To turn the everyday marble cupcakes into a simple family or party showstopper, transfer the batter to a larger bundt tin and serve drizzled with melted white and milk chocolate for an irresistible and indulgent favourite among friends and colleagues.*

**Serves 12–16**

*For the marble ring cake*

350g (12oz) unsalted butter

350g (12oz) golden caster sugar

   7–8 medium eggs, beaten (weigh the eggs to ensure you have the same weight as the butter and sugar: 350g/12 oz)

4 tsp vanilla bean paste

315g (11¼oz) self-raising flour

120ml (4fl oz) milk

35g (1¼oz) cocoa powder

*For the decoration*

200g (7oz) milk chocolate, melted

200g (7oz) white chocolate, melted

## TO MAKE THE MARBLE RING CAKE

1   Preheat the oven to 170°C fan (190°C/375°F/Gas 5) and grease and flour a 25cm (10-inch) bundt tin (or use quick-release spray).

2   Cream the butter and sugar together in a large bowl until pale and fluffy.

3   Add the beaten eggs slowly until fully incorporated.

4   Divide the mixture between 2 bowls. Stir the vanilla bean paste into one of the bowls and then fold in 175g (6oz) of the flour – add milk as necessary to achieve a dropping consistency.

5   To the other bowl, add the remaining flour and the cocoa, sifted together. Add milk as necessary to achieve a dropping consistency.

6   Transfer the batters to separate large piping bags and snip off the ends with scissors (or use tablespoons to fill the tin).

7   Deposit both the vanilla and chocolate cake batter into the tin until just over half full. Swirl with a skewer to achieve a marbling effect.

8   Bake for 45-50 minutes or until risen and golden and a skewer inserted into the centre comes out clean. Remove from the oven and leave to cool in the tin on a wire rack until cool. Turn out and place on a cake plate.

## TO DECORATE THE CAKE

1   Drizzle first with the melted white chocolate and then with the melted milk chocolate for a simple but effective marble cake to share with family and friends.

The cake is best eaten on the day it is made, but can be stored in an airtight container at room temperature and eaten within 2 days.

CUPCAKES

# CARROT CUPCAKES WITH CITRUS DRIZZLE

*Those of you familiar with Little Venice Cake Company will know this is the recipe
I created for the wedding of Pierce Brosnan and Keely Shaye Smith. It is wonderfully
moist, with a delicious blend of carrots, fruit and spices. The Brosnans recently celebrated
their 18th wedding anniversary – so this recipe continues to stand the test of time.
Simply bake, as below, for Everyday or for your Showstopper top with orange cream
cheese frosting and decorate with caramelised walnut praline (see page 30).*

**Makes 12 large or
18 regular cupcakes**

*For the cupcakes*
2 large eggs
150ml (5fl oz) sunflower oil
75g (3oz) golden caster sugar
75g (3oz) light brown sugar
175g (6oz) plain flour
½–1 tbsp ground cinnamon
(be generous with your spices if you
prefer a more spiced carrot cake)
1–2 tsp ground nutmeg
1 tsp bicarbonate of soda
20g stem ginger or 1 tsp ground ginger
grated zest of 1 orange
grated zest of 1 lemon
50g (2oz) chopped walnuts
50g (2oz) desiccated coconut
100g (3½oz) sultanas, washed
175g (6oz) carrots, peeled and grated

*For the drizzle*
75g (3oz) light brown sugar
juice of 1 lemon
juice of 1 orange

**TO MAKE THE CUPCAKES**
1 Preheat the oven to 170°C fan (190°C/375°F/Gas 5) and
place 12 large or 18 regular cupcake cases in cupcake tins.
2 Blend the eggs, oil and sugar together in a large bowl until
well mixed.
3 In a separate bowl, sift the flour, spices and bicarbonate of soda
together and stir into the oil mixture to create a smooth batter.
4 Add the remaining ingredients and mix well.
5 Fill the cupcake cases to two-thirds full. Bake for 15-20 minutes
(depending on the size of your cupcake cases) or until well risen,
golden brown and a skewer inserted in the centre comes out clean.

**TO MAKE THE DRIZZLE**
1 While the cakes are in the oven, prepare the drizzle. Measure the
ingredients into a jug and stir until dissolved.

**TO ASSEMBLE THE CAKES**
1 As soon as the cakes are baked, transfer them to a wire rack, spike
each cake with a skewer and brush over the syrup. Leave the cakes
to cool.

Store the cupcakes in an airtight container in the refrigerator for up to
14 days. Suitable for freezing.

# CARROT CUPCAKES WITH CREAM CHEESE FROSTING AND WALNUT PRALINE

*These cream cheese frosted carrot cupcakes, with crunchy, sweet walnut praline are the ultimate go to when it comes to satisfying, nutritious, delicious cake. Deliciously moist with a subtle spice, the flavour and texture combinations ensure they are a timeless classic.*

**Makes 12 large or**
**18 regular cupcakes**

1 quantity of Carrot Cupcakes (see page 29)

*For the walnut praline*
50g (2oz) walnuts, roughly chopped
100g (3½oz) caster sugar

*For the cream cheese frosting*
450g (1lb) icing sugar
75g (3oz) unsalted butter, chilled
    but removed from the fridge
    30 minutes before using
190g (6½oz) full-fat cream cheese,
    chilled
2 tsp vanilla bean paste
2 tsp orange oil or grated zest of
    1 orange

### TO MAKE THE WALNUT PRALINE

1   Preheat the oven to 170°C fan (190°C/375°F/Gas 5).
2   Place the walnuts on a baking sheet in the oven for 15 minutes until roasted. Remove and leave to cool slightly.
3   Meanwhile, place the sugar in a heavy-based pan over a moderate heat until the sugar melts and turns a warm caramel colour (do not stir it at all – simply swirl the pan).
4   Add the roasted walnuts, swirl until well coated and then transfer to a baking sheet lined with non-stick baking paper. Leave to cool then blitz in a food processor or chop with a knife into small bite-sized pieces.

### TO MAKE THE CREAM CHEESE FROSTING

1   Measure the icing sugar and chilled butter into a stand mixer or food processor. Pulse until the mixture resembles fine breadcrumbs. Add the chilled cream cheese and beat until smooth. Beat in the vanilla bean paste and the orange zest or oil.

### TO ASSEMBLE THE CAKES

1   Fit a large piping bag with a nozzle of your choice and fill will the cream cheese frosting. Pipe a generous portion of cream cheese frosting onto each cupcake and decorate with the chopped walnut praline.

These cakes can be stored for up to 7 days in the refrigerator and are suitable for freezing.

### TOP TIP

If you prefer a salted flavour, sprinkle the walnuts with a teaspoon of sea salt before roasting.

# VANILLA FAIRY CAKES WITH SIMPLE GLACE ICING

*The simplest and easiest entry level for complete beginners has to be the vanilla cupcake or fairy cake. These should still be buttery, light as air and be uniform in size and colour. I have used a very simple glace or water icing and shop-bought toppers for decoration. To all those who say 'I can't bake' – I challenge you with these! For the seasoned baker – these are perfect as the base for many of your cupcake projects.*

**Makes 12 fairy cakes**

*For the fairy cakes*
150g (5oz) unsalted butter, softened
150g (5oz) golden caster sugar
3 large eggs, beaten (weigh the eggs and ensure you have the same weight as the butter, sugar and flour 150g/5oz)
150g (5oz) self-raising flour
30ml (2 tbsp) whole milk
1 tsp vanilla bean paste

*For the glace icing*
200g (7oz) icing sugar
1 tsp vanilla extract

*For the decoration*
12 cake topper decorations

## TO MAKE THE FAIRY CAKES

1  Preheat the oven to 170°C fan (190°C/375°F/Gas 5) and place 12 paper cases in a cupcake tin.
2  Cream the butter and sugar together in an stand mixer until light and fluffy.
3  Add the beaten eggs slowly until fully incorporated.
4  Sift the flour into the batter and fold in with a metal spoon or rubber spatula.
5  Stir in the milk to reach a dropping consistency. Add the vanilla bean paste.
6  Spoon the batter into a large piping bag and snip off the end with scissors. Deposit the batter evenly into the paper cupcake cases until two-thirds full.
7  Bake for 18 minutes until risen, golden brown on the surface and a skewer inserted in the centre comes out clean. Remove from the oven and leave to cool on a wire rack.

## TO MAKE THE GLACE ICING

1  Sift the icing sugar into a bowl. Add the vanilla extract and enough water to create a smooth icing that will flow but not be too runny or thin.

## TO ASSEMBLE THE CAKES

1  Spoon a little icing on top of each cake using a teaspoon. Finish with a cake topper decoration.

The cakes are best eaten on the day they are made.

### TOP TIP

You can also colour the icing with edible gel colours and finish with coloured sprinkles.

# PIGS AND SHEEP CUPCAKES

*We seem to make a huge effort for our pre-school and early years' children's birthdays and quite rightly so. It's all about creating memories and stimulating the imagination. These cupcakes are delightful, cute and bring a great sense of farmyard fun to any party. They can be made ahead of the party for a take home gift, or, dare I say it – if you feel brave enough – supply bowls of marshmallows and buttercream and let the children decorate them themselves!*

**Makes 20 cupcakes**

*For the fairy cakes*

200g (7oz) unsalted butter, softened
200g (7oz) golden caster sugar
4 medium eggs, beaten (weigh the
    eggs to ensure you have the
    same weight as the butter, sugar and
    flour: 200g/7oz)
200g (7oz) self-raising flour
2 tsp vanilla bean paste
30ml (2 tbsp) whole milk

*For the vanilla syrup*

100g (3½oz) golden caster sugar
100ml (3½fl oz) water
2 tsp vanilla extract

*For the buttercream*

250g (9oz) unsalted butter
500g (1lb 2oz) icing sugar
2 tsp vanilla bean paste
1 tbsp milk
20g (4 tsp) freeze-dried strawberry
    powder

*For the decoration*

100g (3½oz) each chocolate, pink,
    white and black fondant sugar paste
200g (7oz) each white and pink
    mini marshmallows
modelling tools (cone tool, ball tool)

## TO MAKE THE FAIRY CAKES

1   Preheat the oven to 170°C fan (190°C/375°F/Gas 5) and place 20 paper cases in a cupcake tin.
2   Using the cake ingredients, follow the instructions on page 33 to make the cake batter.
3   Spoon the batter into a large piping bag and snip off the end with scissors. Deposit the batter evenly into the cupcake cases until they are two-thirds full.
4   Bake for 25 minutes until risen, golden brown on the surface and a skewer inserted in the centre comes out clean.

## TO MAKE THE VANILLA SYRUP

1   Place all the ingredients in a small saucepan and bring gently to the boil. Turn off the heat as soon as the syrup starts to boil and the sugar has dissolved.
2   When the cakes are baked, remove them from the oven. Spike each cake several times with a bamboo skewer or cocktail stick, brush over the vanilla syrup and leave to cool on a wire rack.

## TO MAKE THE BUTTERCREAM

1   Beat the butter and icing sugar together in a large bowl until mixed and then beat in the vanilla bean paste. Add the milk to the buttercream to achieve the desired consistency. Divide the buttercream in half and add the strawberry powder to one portion.

**TOP TIP**

Look for ready made coloured fondant sugar pastes. Many are also nut and gluten-free.

## TO ASSEMBLE THE CAKES

1 Make the sheep and pig decorations with the different coloured fondant sugar pastes.

*For the pig*
— Knead and shape the pink paste into a small ball and gently flatten to a disc. Use a smiley tool to add the cheeky smile.
— To make make the snout, knead and shape a smaller ball of paste and fix in the centre, just over the mouth fixed in position with a little water. Use the tip of a No. 3 nozzle to add the nostrils.
— For the ears, cut a small ball of paste in half and shape. Holding one ear next to the head, use a cone to gently push and fix the ear to the pig's head.
— Roll two small ball of black paste for the eyes and fix in position with a little water.

*For the sheep*
— Knead the chocolate paste into a pear shape, flattened at the larger end. Fix the elongated, shaped ears into position with a little water. Use the tip of a No. 3 nozzle to make the nostrils.
— Mark the eye position with a cone tool and fill with a small ball of white paste, overlaid with a smaller black paste pupil.
— Finally, roll 4 small white balls of paste and fix in position on the sheep's head with a little water.
— Allow the animal heads to firm up for at least one hour – or make up to 1 month ahead and store in an airtight container.

2 Working on one cupcake at a time, spread with either the vanilla (sheep) or strawberry (pig) buttercream.
3 Position the animal head in the centre – with enough space to fit marshmallows around the head and the rest of the cupcake, filling in all the space with marshmallows gently pushed into the buttercream.
4 Repeat until all the cupcakes are decorated and display on a cake stand or present in individual boxes.

Store in an airtight container at room temperature and eat within 3 days. Not suitable for freezing once decorated.

# GO THE WHOLE HOG

*'Squeak Piggy Squeak!' Now isn't this cake just adorable? It was such joy creating this cake – you can't help but smile when you look at it. The head of the pig and the curly tail are made from fondant sugar paste and fixed in position with cocktail sticks. Deceptively simple to achieve yet impressive as a showstopper cake for many a birthday party. Serve this as the main event – with the pig cupcakes as extra cakes for everyone at the party.*

**Serves 16–20 (party-size portions)**

*For the sponge*

275g (10oz) unsalted butter, softened

275g (10oz) golden caster sugar

5 large eggs, beaten (weigh the eggs
    to ensure you have the same
    weight as the butter, sugar and flour:
    275g/10oz)

1 tbsp vanilla bean paste

275g (10oz) self-raising flour

1 tsp baking powder

70ml (3fl oz) whole milk

*For the strawberry buttercream*

250g (9oz) unsalted butter

450g (1lb) icing sugar

35g (1¼oz) freeze-dried strawberry
    powder

2–4 tbsp milk

*For the decoration*

150g (5oz) pink fondant sugar paste
    mixed with 100g (3½oz) gum paste

black fondant paste (for the eyes)

100g (3½oz) pink, red and white
    sprinkles (although it is always good
    to have double the amount you
    require to make it easier to cover
    the cake)

## TO MAKE THE SPONGE

1   Preheat the oven to 160°C fan (180°C/350°F/Gas 4) and spray the inside of a 20cm (8-inch) hemisphere tin with non-stick release spray. Stand the ring of a 15cm (6 inch) round cake tin inside the tin.

2   Cream the butter and sugar together in a large bowl until pale and light. Add the beaten eggs a little at a time until fully incorporated

3   Stir in the vanilla bean paste. Sift in the flour and baking powder and fold into the cake batter with the milk. Spoon into the cake tin and level the surface.

4   Bake for 1 hour 10 minutes until golden brown and a skewer inserted in the centre comes out clean. Transfer to a wire rack to cool for 10 minutes. Turn the cake out and leave to cool.

## TO MAKE THE BUTTERCREAM

1   Cream the butter, sugar, strawberry powder and milk together in a large bowl until light and fluffy.

### TOP TIP

It's a good idea to make the head and tail while the cake is in the oven or cooling to allow the paste enough time to firm up and be easier to handle – but still malleable enough to shape into position.

## TO ASSEMBLE THE CAKE

1 Use a serrated knife or cake wire to slice the cake horizontally into three layers.

2 Fix the base cake in the centre of a 23cm (9-inch) cake board with a little buttercream.

3 Spread the cake with strawberry buttercream and place the next layer on top. Repeat with more buttercream and then fix the top layer in position.

4 Use a small cranked palette knife to spread the remaining buttercream over the whole cake to create a smooth finish. Place in the fridge for 10 minutes to gently firm (but not chill) and then remove and place on a large baking tray.

5 Press the sprinkles all over the cake starting at the base and working your way up and over the cake. Use your cupped hand to gently lift and press the sprinkles into position.

## TO MAKE THE DECORATIONS

1 To make the head – knead and shape the paste to create the face, snout and ears. Use the cone tool to create the nostrils and the base of a large cupcake nozzle to mark the mouth. Roll two small balls of black paste for the eyes and fix these in position. Try to avoid using icing sugar as this will dry the paste out and make it hard to stick. Leave the face to firm for at least 10 minutes before fixing into position. Insert 4 cocktail sticks so they're just poking out of the cake surface and then place the head over the cocktail sticks to fix in position.

2 For the tail – roll a small piece of pink paste into a curly tail shape and insert one-third of a cocktail stick into the end. Leave to firm and then fix into position at the back of the cake

The cake will keep for up to 3 days stored in a cool, dry place.
Suitable for freezing - freeze in a suitable container with a lid. Defrost at room temperature.

**TOP TIP**

Use this same tin and recipe with different buttercream, sprinkles and decorations to create other cute animals – think black sprinkles and a spider face and 8 legs for Halloween, chocolate vermicelli for a teddy bear or white mini pearls and big ears for a bunny.

# RAISING THE BAA

*We couldn't leave the mini sheep cupcakes without a showstopper – meet Sheila! Rather glamorous, isn't she? I've chosen to make her as a chocolate cake, layered and decorated with white chocolate buttercream and finished with a chocolate fondant face. I've used a 2D nozzle to create the wooly swirls – fun to make and impressive to show your hand-piping skills. Another impressive cake that is both achievable and very yummy.*

**Serves 16–20 (party-size portions)**

*For the sponge*

275g (10oz) unsalted butter, softened

275g (10oz) golden caster sugar

5 large eggs, beaten (weigh the eggs
   to ensure you have the same
   weight as the butter and sugar:
   275g/10oz)

40g (1½oz) cocoa powder

235g (8½oz) self-raising flour

1 tsp baking powder

125ml (4fl oz) whole milk

*For the buttercream*

400g (14oz) unsalted butter

800g (1¾lb) icing sugar

250g (9oz) melted white chocolate,
   cooled slightly

*For the decoration*

300g (11oz) chocolate fondant paste

50g (2oz) white fondant paste

20g (¾oz) black fondant paste

cocktail sticks

modelling tools – cone tool, ball tool,
   paintbrush, 2D nozzle and a large
   piping bag

## TO MAKE THE SPONGE

1   Preheat the oven to 160°C fan (180°C/350°F/Gas 4) and spray the inside of a 20cm (8 inch) hemisphere tin with non-stick release spray. Stand inside the ring of a 15cm (6 inch) round cake tin.

2   Follow the instructions on page 37 to make the sponge batter adding the cocoa powder with the flour and baking powder.

3   Spoon into the cake tin and level the surface. Bake for 1 hour 10 minutes until baked and a skewer inserted in the centre comes out clean. Transfer to a wire rack to cool for 10 minutes. Turn the cake out and leave to cool.

## TO MAKE THE BUTTERCREAM

1   Cream the butter, icing sugar and melted white chocolate together in a large bowl until light and fluffy.

## TO ASSEMBLE THE CAKE

1   Use a serrated knife or cake wire to slice the cake horizontally into 3 layers.

2   Fix the base cake in the centre of a 23cm (9-inch) cake board with a little buttercream.

3   Spread the cake with a little more white chocolate buttercream and place the next layer on top. Repeat with more buttercream and then fix the top layer in position. Use a small cranked palette knife to spread a very thin crumb coat of buttercream over the whole cake. Place in the fridge for 20 minutes to firm.

4   Fit a large piping bag with a 2D nozzle and fill with the white chocolate buttercream. Starting at the base of the cake, pipe swirls of buttercream around the edge – working your way up and over the cake to cover it entirely with swirls. Each swirl should start in the centre and work out. Refrigerate to firm the buttercream before positioning the head.

5   To make the head – knead and shape the paste to create the face, ears and white woollen balls. Use the cone tool to create the nostrils. Roll two small balls of white and black paste for the eyes and fix these in position. Try to avoid using icing sugar as this will dry the paste out and make it hard to stick. Leave the face to firm for at least 10 minutes before fixing into position. Insert 4 cocktail sticks so they're just poking out of the cake surface and then place the head over the cocktail sticks to fix in position.

The cake will keep for up to 3 days stored in a cool, dry place. Suitable for freezing – place in a large cake box with a lid and place in the freezer. To defrost, remove from the freezer and allow to come up to room temperature.

# LEMON MERINGUE CUPCAKES

*I love the quintessential combination of classic lemon curd with silky meringue in these gorgeous lemon meringue cupcakes. Effectively impressive, yet deceptively simple – this recipe allows you to channel your inner chef by wielding your blowtorch to gently colour and caramelise the Italian meringue.*

**Makes 12 cupcakes**

*For the cupcakes*

200g (7oz) unsalted butter, softened

200g (7oz) golden caster sugar

4 large eggs, beaten (weigh the eggs
   to ensure you have the same
   weight as the butter, sugar and flour:
   200g/7oz)

grated zest of 2 lemons

200g (7oz) self-raising flour

60–75ml (2½–3fl oz) milk

*For the lemon curd*

grated zest and juice of 4 lemons

100g (3½oz) unsalted butter, chilled
   and cut into 1cm cubes

350g (12oz) golden caster sugar

4 medium eggs, beaten

*For the Italian meringue*

300g (11oz) caster sugar

25g (1oz) glucose syrup

65ml (2½fl oz) water

140g (4½oz) egg whites
   (from 4 medium eggs)

## TO MAKE THE CUPCAKES

1   Preheat the oven to 170°C fan (190°C/375°F/Gas 5) and place the cupcake cases on a baking tray. With the exception of the milk, all of the cupcake ingredients should be at room temperature.

2   Cream together the butter and sugar in a large bowl until pale and light.

3   Add the beaten eggs a little at a time until fully mixed and then stir in the lemon zest.

4   Sift the flour into the mixture and fold with a metal spoon or spatula and then add the milk to achieve a dropping consistency.

5   Spoon about 65g (2½oz) of batter into each cupcake case.

6   Bake for 20-25 minutes until risen, golden brown and a skewer inserted in the centre comes out clean. Remove from the oven and place on a wire rack to cool.

## TO MAKE THE LEMON CURD

1   Place all the ingredients in a medium saucepan and heat over a medium heat until thickened. Do not allow to boil.

2   Pass the curd through a fine sieve and pour into a container with a lid. Place in the fridge and leave to firm up. It will keep for 4 weeks in the fridge.

### TOP TIP

The lemon curd recipe
will make enough to fill 12
cupcakes and a layer cake –
keep any extra in the fridge and
sneak a bit on hot crumpets or
toast for a mid-morning
second breakfast!

### TO MAKE THE ITALIAN MERINGUE

1   Measure the sugar, glucose and water into a saucepan and heat over medium-high heat, stirring gently.
2   Place a sugar thermometer in the sugar solution and stop stirring when the solution reaches 80°C (176°F). Continue heating without stirring until the temperature reaches 110°C (230°F).
3   Put the egg whites into the bowl of a stand mixer fitted with the whisk attachment. Start whisking on full speed. As the syrup reaches 119°C (246°F) remove the pan from the heat and, with the egg whites still on full speed add the syrup to the egg whites in a slow, steady stream.
4   Once all the syrup has been added, whisk until the meringue has cooled to room temperature – it will thicken and be wonderfully glossy, white and stiff.

### TO ASSEMBLE THE CUPCAKES

1   Use a cupcake corer or sharp paring knife to remove the centre of each cupcake, keeping the plug of cake.
2   Fill the hole with a generous 2 teaspoons of lemon curd and replace the plug of sponge.
3   Fit a large piping bag with a plain nozzle and fill with the Italian meringue. Starting in the centre of the cupcake, pipe a circle swirl of meringue to the outside of the cupcake and then continue upwards and inwards finishing with a gentle curl at the top.
4   Gently colour and caramelise the meringue with a blowtorch.

Serve at room temperature. The cupcakes can be kept for up to 3 days in the refrigerator.

### TOP TIPS

— To save time, use a jar of ready-made lemon curd.

— Fill a large piping bag with the cake batter. Snip off the end and use to fill the cupcake cases for a professional, clean finish. You can even weigh each one to ensure you deposit exactly the same weight in each.

— Be careful not to take the blowtorch too close to the meringue. Keep it moving from side to side.

— Replace the homemade Italian meringue with ready-made meringues and place one on top of each of the finished cupcakes.

# LEMON MERINGUE LAYER CAKE

*For a special garden party or summer celebration this lemon meringue layer cake is a certain showstopper. Perfect your hand-piping skills by piping a double row of roses around the side of the cake and fill the top with fresh seasonal berries – I have chosen blackberries and the super-sweet seedless black Vitoria grapes, delicately finished with fresh lavender sprigs from the garden.*

**Serves 12–16**

*For the sponges*

275g (10oz) unsalted butter, softened

275g (10oz) golden caster sugar

4 large eggs, beaten (weigh the eggs to ensure you have the same weight as the butter, sugar and flour: 275g/10oz)

grated zest of 3 lemons

275g (10oz) self-raising flour

70–100ml (3–3½fl oz) milk

*For the filling*

1 quantity of Lemon Curd (see page 44)

*For the decoration*

1 quantity of Italian Meringue (see page 46)

seasonal berries, grapes and lavender sprigs

## TOP TIP

The egg white in the meringue is cooked by the heat of the sugar syrup so it is stable and safe to eat at room temperature. Use the meringue straight away after it has been made – it cannot be re-whisked.

## TO MAKE THE SPONGES

1   Preheat the oven to 160°C fan (180°C/350°F/Gas 4) and grease and line the base and sides of three 20cm (8 inch) round, loose-bottom sandwich cake tins.

2   Use the sponge ingredients to make the batter following the instructions on page 44. Divide the batter equally between the tins (place each on the scales and weigh the batter into each tin).

3   Bake for 20-25 minutes until risen, golden brown and a skewer inserted in the centre comes out clean.

4   Remove from the oven and place on a wire rack. Leave to cool in the tin for 10 minutes until turning out onto the wire rack to cool.

## TO ASSEMBLE THE CAKE

1   Place the first layer of sponge on a large cake stand. Fit a large piping bag with a plain nozzle and fill with Italian meringue (or use a small palette knife). Pipe a ring of meringue around the outer edge of the cake to act as a wall.

2   Spoon 3 tablespoons of lemon curd on top of the cake, inside the wall of meringue and level. Place the next layer on top and repeat the process.

3   Finish with the top layer and then use a palette knife to create a crumb coat of meringue all over the cake. The sides can be barely coated, but you can afford to be more generous with the layer on top.

4   Fit a large piping bag with a 2D nozzle and fill with the meringue. Start at the base of the cake and pipe a ring of roses around the base of the cake finishing with a swirl at the top of each rose.

5   Repeat with the upper row, ensuring the top of the rose finishes just higher than the cake itself.

6   Gently colour and caramelise the roses and top of the cake with a blowtorch. Fill the centre of the cake with fresh seasonal berries, grapes and lavender to finish.

Serve at room temperature. The cake will keep for 2 days stored uncovered in the fridge.

# GIN AND TONIC CUPCAKES

*To get you in the party mood, these adult cupcakes are heavenly delicious.*
*I have brushed the freshly baked lime cupcakes with a gin and tonic syrup*
*and then decorated them with a gin and fresh lime buttercream.*
*To your very good health!*

**Makes 12 cupcakes**

*For the cupcakes*

200g (7oz) unsalted butter, at
     room temperature

200g (7oz) golden caster sugar

4 large eggs, beaten (weigh the eggs
     to ensure you have the same
     weight as the butter, sugar and
     flour: 200g/7oz)

200g (7oz) self-raising flour

2 tbsp gin

grated zest of 2 limes

*For the gin and tonic syrup*

50g (2oz) golden caster sugar

50ml (2fl oz) tonic water

2 tbsp gin

*For the gin and fresh lime buttercream*

250g (9oz) unsalted butter

500g (1lb 2oz) superfine icing sugar
     (cornflour-free)

grated zest of 2 limes

25ml (1oz) gin

20ml (¾fl oz) lime juice

*For the decoration*

blueberries

mint leaves

mini Refreshers sherbet sweets

paper straws

## TO MAKE THE CUPCAKES

1   Preheat the oven to 170°C fan (190°C/375°F/Gas 5) and place
    12 cupcake cases in a cupcake tin.
2   Beat the butter and sugar together in a large bowl until
    light and fluffy. Add the beaten eggs a little at a time until fully
    incorporated. Sift the flour into the cake mixture. Stir in the gin
    and lime zest.
3   Transfer the batter into a large piping bag and snip off the end.
    Deposit 65g (2½oz) batter into each cupcake case and bake for
    25 minutes until golden and a skewer inserted into the centre
    comes out clean. Transfer to a wire rack.

## TO MAKE THE SYRUP

1   Meanwhile, make the syrup – heat together the sugar and tonic
    water in a small pan. Boil for 1 minute and then remove from the
    heat. Stir in the gin. Spike the cupcakes with a skewer and brush
    the top of the cupcakes with the syrup. Leave to cool.

## TO MAKE THE BUTTERCREAM

1   Beat the ingredients together in a large bowl until smooth and
    creamy.
2   Fit a piping bag with a large 195C open-star-nozzle, fill with
    the buttercream, and pipe a generous swirl of buttercream on
    each cupcake.
3   Decorate with fresh blueberries, mint leaves, refresher sherbet
    sweets and colourful paper straws.

These cupcakes are best enjoyed on
the day they are made – not suitable
for freezing. Store in a cake box
if necessary.

**TOP TIP**

Place the paper cases on
a set of scales and deposit
the correct weight into each
case to ensure every cake
bakes evenly.

# GIN AND TONIC PARTY CAKE

*This summer showstopper spectacular is made up of four layers of super-light, fresh lime sponge brushed with gin and tonic syrup. I've layered the sponge with alternate layers of blueberry and gin and lime buttercreams with fresh blueberries to balance the flavour. I've simply textured the buttercream around the sides and top of the cake to create an ombre finish and decorated the cake with hand-piped buttercream, cucumber, lime and Refreshers sherbet sweets.*

**Serves 12–16**

*For the sponge*

60g (2½oz) unsalted butter,
    melted, plus extra for brushing

8 medium eggs

230g (8¼oz) golden caster sugar

2 tbsp vanilla bean paste

230g (8¼oz) self-raising flour

grated zest of 4 limes

*For the gin and tonic syrup*

75g (3oz) golden caster sugar

75ml (3fl oz) tonic water

3 tbsp gin

*For the gin and fresh lime buttercream*

125g (4oz) unsalted butter,
    at room temperature

250g (9oz) superfine icing sugar
    (cornflour-free)

grated zest of 2 limes

25ml (1fl oz) gin

20ml (¾fl oz) lime juice

*For the blueberry buttercream*

125g (4oz) unsalted butter, at
    room temperature

250g (9oz) superfine icing sugar
    (cornflour-free)

25g (1oz) freeze-dried blueberry
    powder

## TO MAKE THE SPONGE

1   Preheat the oven to 180°C fan (200°C/400°F/Gas 6). Line two 20 x 30cm (8 x 12 inch) Swiss roll tins with baking paper and brush with melted butter.

2   Place the eggs and sugar in a large bowl placed over a large saucepan of gently simmering water. Whisk with a handheld electric whisk until tripled in size, light, aerated and the batter leaves a thick trail.

3   Remove from the heat and stir in the vanilla bean paste and the melted butter. Sift in the flour and fold into the mixture until fully incorporated. Stir in the lime zest. Divide the batter between the 2 tins and spread the mixture out with the back of a spoon – evenly and into the corners.

4   Bake for 12 minutes until risen, gently golden and the top springs back when lightly pressed.

5   Turn the sponges out onto a sheet of non-stick baking parchment placed on a cooling rack and leave to cool.

## TO MAKE THE SYRUP AND BUTTERCREAMS

1   Follow the instructions on page 51.

→

### TOP TIP

Choose your favourite local flavoured gin to ring the changes with this recipe – pink grapefruit, rhubarb and raspberry gin are all excellent choices.

CUPCAKES

*For the decoration*

2 mini cucumbers, thinly sliced
    lengthways

200g (7oz) blueberries

lime wedges

mini Refreshers sherbet sweets

**TO ASSEMBLE THE CAKE**

1   Brush the sponges generously with the gin and tonic syrup.
    Cut the 2 sponges in half lengthways to create 4 rectangular
    sponges, each one measuring 10 x 30cm (5 x 12 inches).

2   Lay the first sponge on a plate or tray and spread the blueberry
    buttercream over the top with a palette knife. Sprinkle generously
    with fresh blueberries (about 50g/2oz).

3   Place the next layer of sponge on top and press down. Spread
    with gin and lime buttercream and sprinkle with another 50g
    (2oz) blueberries. Repeat with the next sponge and blueberry
    buttercream and blueberries before placing the final sponge layer
    on top. Press down.

4   Spread more blueberry buttercream generously around the lower
    third section of the cake. Spread the gin and lime buttercream
    around the sides and top and smooth with a palette knife to blend
    the buttercreams together.

5   Fit a piping bag with a large 195C open-star-nozzle and the lime
    buttercream. Hand pipe generous swirls of buttercream on the top
    of the cake and decorate with fresh cucumber slices, blueberries,
    limes wedges and Refreshers sherbet sweets.

This cake is best enjoyed on the day it is made – not suitable for
freezing. Store in a cake box if necessary.

**TOP TIP**

This is a whisked sponge with
very little butter. Brush the sponges
generously with the syrup to make the
cake nice and moist. The acidity of
the fresh blueberries cuts through the
sweetness of the buttercream
to balance this cake with a
wonderful flavour.

# STRAWBERRY AND ORANGE CUPCAKES

*If I were to say 'summer' – would you immediately think strawberries and cream? These gorgeously fragrant orange cupcakes are decorated with a strawberry buttercream and then finished with a white chocolate drip and fresh strawberries. Perfect for all your Wimbledon-inspired parties, al-fresco lunches, local village fetes and cricket afternoon teas.*

**Makes 12 cupcakes**

*For the cupcakes*

175g (6oz) unsalted butter, softened, at room temperature

175g (6oz) golden caster sugar

3 large eggs (weigh the eggs to ensure you have the same weight as the butter, sugar and flour: the same weight as the butter, sugar and flour: 175g/6oz)

grated zest of 2 oranges

2 tsp orange oil

2 tsp vanilla extract

175g (6oz) self-raising flour

80ml (3fl oz) milk

*For the white chocolate drip*

75ml (3fl oz) double cream

225g (8oz) white chocolate, broken into pieces

Super white colouring (optional)

*For the Swiss meringue buttercream*

115ml (3½fl oz) egg whites

200g (7oz) golden caster sugar

250g (9oz) unsalted butter, chilled but removed from the fridge 30 minutes before using)

2 tsp vanilla extract

25g (1oz) freeze-dried strawberry powder

## TO MAKE THE CUPCAKES

1 Preheat the oven to 170°C fan (190°C/375°F/Gas 5) and line a tray with cupcake cases.

2 Cream the butter and sugar together in a large bowl until pale and fluffy.

3 Beat the eggs in a jug and then pour into the creamed mixture slowly until fully incorporated.

4 Stir in the orange zest, orange oil and vanilla extract.

5 Sift in the flour and fold into the mixture. Add the milk as necessary to create a dropping consistency.

6 Spoon the batter into a large piping bag and snip off the end. Deposit 75g (3oz) batter into each cupcake case (weigh as you go) to ensure every cupcake is even.

7 Bake for 25 minutes until risen, golden and a skewer inserted in the centre comes out clean.

8 Remove from the oven and place on a wire rack to cool.

## TO MAKE THE WHITE CHOCOLATE DRIP

1 Mix the cream and white chocolate together in a large heatproof bowl.

2 Heat in the microwave gently until the white chocolate has fully melted and the mixture is smooth. Add a few drops of super white colouring to make the drip white and opaque, if liked.

### TOP TIP

Snip off the very end of the strawberry stalks before decorating to leave a clean, neat finish. Chill the buttercreamed cakes before applying the chocolate drip to allow the frosting to firm up.

**TO MAKE THE SWISS MERINGUE BUTTERCREAM**

1  Heat the egg whites and the sugar together in a heatproof bowl over a pan of gently simmering water, stirring all the time until the egg/sugar temperature reaches 65-71°C (149-160°F).
2  Remove from the heat and transfer the bowl to a stand mixer. Using the whisk attachment, whisk the egg and sugar until a thick glossy meringue forms and the meringue cools.
3  Change the whisk attachment for the beater and add the chilled butter in small cubes until fully incorporated and thick. Add the vanilla extract and the strawberry powder to taste.

**TO ASSEMBLE THE CUPCAKES**

1  Use a small palette knife to generously spread buttercream on top of each cupcake and create a small well on the top to hold the white chocolate and fresh strawberry.
2  Fill a small piping bag with the warm chocolate drip icing. Snip-off off the end and carefully pipe a pool and drip on each cupcake. Nestle a strawberry into the chocolate icing to decorate.

These cakes will keep for 2-3 days - store in a refrigerator but eat at room temperature.

# SECRET HEART STRAWBERRY AND ORANGE LAYER CAKE

*This showstopper cake features a heart-filled fresh orange cake, covered with strawberry Swiss meringue buttercream and a white chocolate drip. To finish I have decorated the cake with hand-decorated macarons, fresh fruit and dried rose buds – it's like a secret garden in a secret heart cake!*

**Makes 1 x 25cm (10 inch) cake**

*For the sponge*

melted butter, for greasing

360g (12½oz) unsalted butter, softened at room temperature

360g (12½oz) golden caster sugar

6 large eggs (weigh the eggs to ensure you have the same weight as the butter, sugar and flour: 360g/12½oz)

360g (12½oz) self-raising flour

grated zest of 2 oranges

2 tsp orange oil

2 tsp vanilla extract

100ml (3½fl oz) milk

*For the decoration*

2 quantities of Strawberry Swiss Meringue Buttercream (see page 58)

1 quantity of White Chocolate Drip (see page 57)

selection of fresh fruits

macarons

dried rose buds

small sugar pearls

## TO MAKE THE SPONGE

1  Preheat the oven to 170°C fan (190°C/375°F/Gas 5). Brush two 25cm (10-inch) round, heart fill cake tins with melted butter.

2  Cream the butter and sugar together until pale and fluffy.

3  Beat the eggs in a jug and then pour them into the creamed mixture slowly until fully incorporated.

4  Sift in the flour and fold in. Add the orange zest, orange oil and vanilla extract and continue to fold until the mixture is smooth. Add enough milk to create a dropping consistency if needed.

5  Transfer to the 2 tins – one tin is deeper than the other so allow for this – and smooth the tops. Bake for 30-35 minutes (the deeper cake may need the extra 5 minutes), until risen and golden.

6  Remove the tins from the oven and leave the cakes to cool in the tins on a wire rack. Remove from the tins, wrap loosely in cling film and chill to firm before filling.

## TO ASSEMBLE THE CAKE

1  Trim the very top of both cakes (where the heart is to be filled). Fill a piping bag with buttercream and snip off the end. Fill each half of the heart on the cakes and level with a small palette knife.

2  Place the bottom half on a large sheet of baking paper on a tray. Immediately turn the top layer on top and settle into position.

3  Use a palette knife to spread buttercream over the top and sides of the cake and smooth with a scraper to create smooth, flat sides and top.

4  Chill for 15-30 minutes until firm to the touch. Repeat with a second layer of buttercream to ensure the cake is evenly covered.

5  Transfer the cake to a stand. Fill a piping bag with the white chocolate drip and drip around the edges of the cake. Fill the top and smooth over. Decorate with fruits, macarons, rose buds and pearls.

This cake will keep for 2-3 days - store in the refrigerator but eat at room temperature.

# BLACK FOREST CHERRY CUPCAKES

*Chocolate and cherries have long enjoyed a well-established affinity so I have chosen to include these cheerful cupcakes with a plumped-up black cherry jam filling and a lighter, fresh chocolate cream. They are perfect for those who prefer a smooth, less sweet cupcake – for any time of every day!*

**Makes 12 cupcakes**

*For the cupcakes*
200g (7oz) unsalted butter, softened
200g (7oz) light brown sugar
4 medium eggs, beaten (weigh the
    eggs to ensure you have the same
    weight as the butter and sugar:
    200g/7oz)
170g (6oz) self-raising flour
30g (1¼oz) cocoa powder
60ml (2½fl oz) milk

*For the chocolate cream*
50g (2oz) dark chocolate
    (70% cocoa solids)
35ml (1½fl oz) water
300ml (10fl oz) double cream
40g (1½oz) golden caster sugar
1 tsp vanilla bean paste

*For the decoration*
300g (10oz) black cherry conserve
12 fresh cherries
chocolate shavings (use a vegetable
    peeler along the edge of a bar of
    dark chocolate to make chocolate
    shavings)

## TO MAKE THE CUPCAKES
1   Preheat the oven to 170°C fan (190°C/375°F/Gas 5) and place 12 cupcake cases in a shallow baking tin.
2   Cream the butter and sugar together in a large bowl until pale and fluffy.
3   Add the beaten egg a little at a time until fully incorporated.
4   Sift the flour and cocoa together into the batter and fold in carefully with a metal spoon or rubber spatula. Stir in the milk to achieve a dropping consistency.
5   Spoon the batter into a large piping bag and snip off the end. Deposit 70g (3oz) of batter into each cupcake case (or adjust if you are using different size cases – the cases should be two-thirds full).
6   Bake for 20-25 minutes until risen and baked through. Remove from the oven and place on a wire rack to cool.

## TO MAKE THE CHOCOLATE CREAM
1   Place the chocolate and water in a saucepan and heat gently until completely melted and smooth. Remove from the heat and cool.
2   Whip the cream together with the sugar and vanilla bean paste in a large bowl. As the cream begins to thicken, add the melted chocolate. The chocolate cream is likely to thicken quickly so be vigilant!

## TO ASSEMBLE THE CUPCAKES
1   When you are ready to fill and decorate the cupcakes, use a cupcake corer to remove the centre of each cupcake and keep to one side.
2   Spoon a very generous teaspoon of black cherry conserve into each cupcake and then replace the plug of cake and gently press down.
3   Fit a large piping bag with a star nozzle and spoon in the chocolate cream. Starting in the centre of each cupcake, pipe a swirl of cream round to the outer edge and then upwards and inwards to a point. Finish with a sprinkle of chocolate shavings a fresh cherry.

These cakes should be kept refrigerated and eaten within 3 days.

# BLACK FOREST ROULADE

*For a showstopper I have turned this everyday hero into a regal roulade. I think it looks quite resplendent with its deliciously tempting chocolate cream and cherry filling and uniform fresh cherry decoration. Roulades are much simpler to make than you may think – so this light, gluten-free roulade is a winner when it comes to an impressive cake that can easily be served as pudding.*

**Serves 6–8**

*For the roulade*
melted butter, for brushing
6 large eggs, separated
150g (5oz) golden caster sugar, plus
    1 tbsp to sprinkle
50g (2oz) cocoa powder

*For the filling*
1 quantity of Chocolate Cream
    (see page 63)
300g (10oz) black cherry conserve

*For the decoration*
12 fresh cherries
chocolate shavings

**TO MAKE THE ROULADE**

1   Preheat the oven to 170°C fan (190°C/375°F/Gas 5). Line the base and sides of a 33 x 23cm (13 x 9 inch) roulade tin with baking paper and brush lightly with melted butter.

2   Place the sugar and egg yolks in a large heatproof bowl over a pan of simmering water and whisk until light, pale and it leaves a ribbon trail. Remove from the heat.

3   Sift the cocoa powder over the mixture and fold in using a spatula.

4   Whisk the egg whites until firm peaks just form and mix 2 large spoonfuls into the chocolate mixture until mixed and slackened. Carefully fold in the remaining egg white with a metal spoon until fully mixed.

5   Transfer the batter to the prepared tin, levelling the mixture into the corners with the back of a spoon.

6   Bake for 20 minutes until firm to the touch.

7   Remove the roulade from the oven and immediately turn out onto a fresh sheet of baking paper sprinkled with golden caster sugar on a cold, damp tea towel. Carefully peel the back of the paper away from the roulade. Roll the roulade up with the fresh piece of paper inside the roulade, the tea towel on the outside. Leave to cool and then chill.

CUPCAKES

**TO ASSEMBLE THE CAKE**

1  When you are ready to fill the roulade, unroll the sponge but keep
   it on the baking paper. Reserve 2 large tablespoons of chocolate
   cream in a piping bag fitted with a plain nozzle.

2  Use a palette knife to spread the remaining cream over the surface
   to the edges of the roulade. Spoon the black cherry compote over
   the cream layer and spread with a palette knife.

3  Roll the roulade up carefully, using the baking paper to help
   roll and keep everything together. Transfer the roulade onto a
   presentation plate using the paper, with the seam of the roulade
   underneath, and then carefully remove the paper.

4  Pipe the remaining cream on top of the roulade and
   decorate with the fresh cherries. Sprinkle with the chocolate
   shavings to finish.

The roulade can be kept refrigerated for up to 3 days. Suitable for
freezing (without the fresh cherries). Place in a large container with a
lid and freeze. Transfer to the refrigerator to defrost.

# LOAF CAKES, TRAYBAKES AND MERINGUES

# WARMING GINGER LOAF CAKE

*As soon as you mention ginger cake, I think warming, rich, spiced cake with sticky, tickly, caramelised undertones and this cake certainly delivers. For this everyday loaf cake I have added a ginger syrup poured over the cake as it is baked warm. It would be just plain rude not to serve it with a scoop of vanilla ice cream, too.*

**Makes 1 x 2lb loaf cake**

*For the cake*

60g (2½oz) unsalted butter, plus
    extra melted for greasing

125g (4oz) golden syrup

1 large egg, beaten

125ml (4fl oz) milk

125g (4oz) plain flour

1 tsp bicarbonate of soda

½ tsp baking powder

pinch of salt

1 heaped tsp ground ginger

½ tsp mixed spice

100g (3½oz) soft brown sugar

40g (1½oz) finely chopped stem ginger

*For the syrup*

2 tbsp syrup from stem ginger

2 tbsp golden caster sugar

30g (1¼oz) chopped stem ginger

juice of ½ lemon or 1 lime

*To serve*

vanilla ice cream

**TO MAKE THE CAKE**

1   Preheat the oven to 160°C fan (180°C/350°F/Gas 4). Grease and line a 900g (2lb) loaf tin.
2   Melt the butter and golden syrup together in a saucepan over a medium heat until melted. Remove from the heat and then add the egg and milk and stir until smooth
3   Sift the flour, bicarbonate of soda, baking powder, salt and spices into a bowl. Stir in the sugar.
4   Make a well in the centre, pour the liquid into the centre of the dry ingredients and mix until smooth. Stir in the chopped ginger
5   Pour the batter into the prepared tin and bake for 20 minutes until risen and firm to the touch. Leave to cool for 5 minutes in the tin before turning out onto a wire rack to cool.

**TO MAKE THE SYRUP**

1   Meanwhile, make the syrup for the loaf by placing all the ingredients in a small saucepan and gently warming through until dissolved and thickened.
2   Spoon over the cake and serve thick warm slices of cake with vanilla ice cream. Any additional syrup can be served on the side.

The cake will keep for 3–5 days in a suitable sealed container. Suitable for freezing.

# GINGER CAKES WITH LIME BUTTERCREAM AND PINEAPPLE SUNFLOWERS

*It's nice to put a little more care and attention into individual cakes and these tropical cakes certainly showcase additional patience and skill. I've baked the ginger cakes inside individual mould tins with removable bases – quite clever and time-saving! The cakes form a natural crust on the top so turn them upside down to decorate – using fresh lime buttercream and effective golden pineapple sunflowers.*

**Makes 12 cakes**

1 quantity Warming Ginger Loaf Cake mixture (see page 71)

*For the fresh lime buttercream*
200g (7oz) unsalted butter
400g (14oz) icing sugar
grated zest of 3 limes
juice of 2 limes

*For the pineapple sunflowers*
1 small pineapple, trimmed, peeled and cut into the thinnest rounds possible
gold lustre spray

## TOP TIP

Cut the pineapple as thinly as possible and dry thoroughly before placing in the oven. Alternatively you could use ready-made dried banana chips!

### TO MAKE THE CAKES

1. Preheat the oven to 160°C fan (180°C/350°F/Gas 4). Brush the insides of a 12-hole removable-base cake tin with melted butter (or spray with quick-release spray).
2. Divide the ginger cake mixture equally among the 12 holes (about 40g/1½oz in each) and bake for 40 minutes until risen and firm to the touch. Leave to cool for 5 minutes in the tin before turning out onto a wire rack to cool.

### TO MAKE THE FRESH LIME BUTTERCREAM

1. Blend all the ingredients together until smooth and light.

### TO MAKE THE PINEAPPLE SUNFLOWERS

1. Preheat the oven to 90°C fan (110°C/225°F/Gas ¼).
2. Pat the pineapple slices dry with kitchen paper. Line 2 baking sheets with non-stick baking paper and lay the pineapple slices on top. Bake for 1½–2 hours, turning the pineapple over every 30 minutes, until the pieces are slightly shrunken and dry.
3. Transfer the pineapple pieces to the wells of a cupcake tin to encourage the pineapple to set in the flower shape and return to the oven for 5-10 minutes until they are dry and the edges are starting to curl. Leave to cool in the tin, then spray with gold lustre.

### TO ASSEMBLE THE CAKES

1. Once the cakes are baked and cooled, turn them upside down – they will be quite sticky.
2. Fit a large piping bag with a star nozzle and fill with the lime buttercream. Pipe a generous swirl of buttercream on the top of each cake and press a pineapple flower on the top at an angle so they are all facing in one direction – a little like natural sunflowers in a field when they all turn to worship the sun.

The cakes will keep in a container with a lid for up to 3 days.

# RASPBERRY AND WHITE CHOCOLATE TRAYBAKE

*This soft cake has a wonderful flavour of raspberries – combining fresh with freeze-dried powder for an enhanced flavour. I have topped the cake with a creamy white chocolate ganache, decorated with freeze-dried raspberries. This is a wonderfully fresh, somewhat sophisticated cake that is rather lovely for breakfast – for which I give you permission!*

**Serves 12**

*For the white chocolate ganache*
100ml (3½fl oz) double cream
300g (11oz) white chocolate chips

*For the traybake*
125g (4oz) raspberries
35g (1¼oz) freeze-dried raspberry powder
65ml (2½fl oz) whole milk
300g (11oz) unsalted butter, softened
300g (11oz) golden caster sugar
5 large eggs (weigh the eggs to ensure you have the same weight as the butter, sugar and flour: 300g/11oz)
300g (11oz) self-raising flour
1 tsp baking powder

*For the decoration*
5g (1 tsp) freeze-dried raspberries

## TO MAKE THE WHITE CHOCOLATE GANACHE

1   Mix the cream and white chocolate together in a large heatproof bowl. Heat in the microwave gently until the white chocolate has fully melted and the mixture is smooth. Cover in cling film and place in the fridge to chill overnight.

## TO MAKE THE TRAYBAKE

1   Preheat the oven to 170°C fan (190°C/375°F/Gas 5) and line the base and sides of a 20 x 30cm (8 x 12 inch) traybake tin with non-stick baking paper.
2   Place the raspberries in a bowl and crush with the back of a spoon or fork. Press through a sieve to remove the pips. Stir in the raspberry powder and milk until smooth and set aside.
3   Cream the butter and sugar together in a large bowl until pale and fluffy.
4   Beat the eggs in a jug and then pour into the creamed mixture slowly until fully incorporated.
5   Sift in the flour and baking powder and fold in. Add the raspberry mixture and continue to fold until the cake mixture is smooth.
6   Transfer the mixture to the tin. Smooth the top and then bake for 40 minutes until baked, risen and golden. Remove the tin from the oven and leave the cake to cool in the tin on a wire rack.

## TO DECORATE THE TRAYBAKE

1   Remove the ganache 30 minutes before you are ready to decorate the cake. Use an electric hand whisk to whip the ganache until light and fluffy.
2   Use a palette knife to spread white chocolate ganache over the top of the cake and sprinkle with freeze-dried raspberries.
3   Place in the fridge to firm up and then cut into 12 generous squares.

This cake will keep for 2–3 days - store in the refrigerator but best consumed at room temperature. Suitable for freezing.

# FAB RASPBERRY AND WHITE CHOCOLATE HEART CAKE

*To ramp up the raspberry and white chocolate traybake into a showstopper, I have used special hidden heart-centre tins and filled the cake with white chocolate ganache. The top and sides of the cake are decorated with colourful sprinkles which make you smile. The combination of fresh raspberry and white chocolate is heavenly – the ganache gives a wonderful creaminess to this cake without being overly sweet.*

**Serves 12–16**

*For the sponges*

melted butter, for brushing

150g (5oz) raspberries

40g (1½oz) freeze-dried raspberry powder

75ml (3fl oz) whole milk

360g (12½oz) unsalted butter, softened at room temperature

360g (12½oz) golden caster sugar

6 large eggs (weigh the eggs to ensure you have the same weight as the butter, sugar and flour: 360g/12½oz)

360g (12½oz) self-raising flour

1 tsp baking powder

*For the white chocolate ganache*

300ml (10fl oz) double cream

900g (1lb) white chocolate chips

*For the decoration*

250g (9oz) mulit-coloured sprinkles

## TO MAKE THE SPONGES

1   Preheat the oven to 170°C fan (190°C/375°F/Gas 5) and brush a twin set of 25cm (10-inch) round, heart fill cake tins generously with melted butter.

2   Place the raspberries in a bowl and crush with the back of a spoon or fork. Press through a sieve to remove the pips. Stir in the raspberry powder and milk until smooth and set aside.

3   Cream the butter and sugar together in a large bowl until pale and fluffy.

4   Beat the eggs in a jug and then pour into the creamed mixture slowly until fully incorporated.

5   Sift the flour and baking powder into the batter and fold in to incorporate. Add the raspberry mixture and continue to fold until the mixture is smooth. Transfer into the two tins – one tin is deeper than the other so allow for this.

6   Smooth the tops and then bake for 30–35 minutes until baked (the deeper cake may take an extra 5 minutes), risen and golden.

7   Remove the tins from the oven and leave the cakes to cool in the tins on a wire rack. Remove from the tins, wrap loosely in cling film and chill to firm before filling.

## TO MAKE THE WHITE CHOCOLATE GANACHE

1   Mix the cream and white chocolate together in a large heatproof bowl.

2   Heat in the microwave gently until the white chocolate has fully melted and the mixture is smooth. Cover in cling film and place in the fridge to chill overnight.

LOAF CAKES, TRAYBAKES AND MERINGUES

**TO ASSEMBLE THE CAKE**

1   Remove the ganache 30 minutes before you are ready to fill the cake.

2   When you are ready to fill the cake, trim the very top of both cakes (where the heart is to be filled).

3   Use an electric hand whisk to whip the ganache until light and fluffy. Fill a piping bag with ganache and snip off the end. Fill each half of the heart on the cakes and level with a small palette knife.

4   Place the bottom half on a large sheet of baking paper on a tray. Immediately turn the top layer over and settle into position.

5   Use a palette knife to spread white chocolate ganache over the top and sides of the cake and smooth with a scraper to create smooth, flat sides and top. Chill for 15 minutes.

6   Repeat with a second layer of ganache to ensure the cake is evenly covered and you can't see any cake through the ganache.

7   Cover the top and sides with sprinkles by gently pressing into the ganache. Use a smoother to create a professional finish.

8   Place in the fridge until firm before removing from the paper and serving on a cake stand. Serve at room temperature.

This cake will keep for 2-3 days - store in the refrigerator but eat at room temperature. Suitable for freezing in a sealed container.

# SALTED CARAMEL POPCORN LOAF CAKE

*When exactly did our love affair with salted caramel start? One thing is for sure –
it is here to stay and for many, the more salted caramel the better! This cake certainly
delivers. I have created a deliciously soft cake, with a decadent salted caramel that
is poured over the loaf cake and served warm. The salted caramel itself can be served
warm over ice cream or poured over our lovely profiterole tower on page 91.*

**Makes 1 x 900g (2lb) loaf cake**

*For the cake*

200g (7oz) salted butter, softened

200g (7oz) light brown muscovado
    sugar

4 medium eggs, beaten (weigh the
    eggs and to ensure you have the
    same weight as the butter, sugar
    and flour: 200g/7oz)

2 tsp vanilla extract

200g (7oz) self-raising flour

50ml (2fl oz) milk

*For the salted caramel*

50g (2oz) caster sugar

100ml (3½fl oz) water

150ml (5fl oz) double cream

15g (½oz) unsalted butter

½ tsp vanilla bean paste

pinch of sea salt

*For the decoration*

toffee popcorn

*To serve*

vanilla ice cream (optional)

**TO MAKE THE CAKE**

1   Preheat the oven to 170°C fan (190°C/375°F/Gas 5). Grease and
    line the base and sides of a 900g (2lb) loaf tin.
2   Cream the butter and sugar together in a large bowl until pale and
    fluffy. Add the beaten egg a little at a time until fully incorporated.
    Stir in the vanilla extract.
3   Sift in the flour and fold with a metal spoon. Stir in the milk.
4   Spoon the batter into the tin and level the surface. Bake for 55
    minutes until risen and golden brown. Remove from the oven and
    leave to cool in the tin for 10 minutes before turning out and leaving
    to cool on a wire rack.

**TO MAKE THE SALTED CARAMEL**

1   Place the sugar and water together in a heavy-based non-stick
    frying pan. Heat until the sugar has dissolved and continue until
    the liquid has coloured to a dark amber. The bubbles will get
    larger, stickier and slower.
2   With caution, add half the cream and whisk into the sugar.
    Reduce the heat and simmer for 2 minutes.
3   Add the remaining cream, butter, vanilla and salt and simmer
    until the caramel has thickened and is no longer cloudy. This may
    take 5-10 minutes. It suddenly will appear clearer and shiny –
    this is the point you're looking for! Pour into a clean bowl or jug
    and leave to cool. Taste and add more salt if necessary.

**TO ASSEMBLE THE CAKE**

1   Place the loaf on a cake plate and spike with a bamboo skewer.
    Pour the warm caramel over the cake until fully drenched.
    Decorate with toffee popcorn. Serve in thick wedges – naturally
    with a bucket of vanilla ice cream!

This cake is best eaten on the day it is made. It will keep for 3 days in a
suitable container stored somewhere cool and dry.

# SALTED CARAMEL AND POPCORN LAYER CAKE

*For this showstopper salted caramel cake, I have baked the cake as three layers and sandwiched them with a salted caramel buttercream. Use your decorating skills to cover the top and sides with smooth buttercream, drip with salted caramel and pile high with toffee popcorn.*

**Makes 1 x 20cm (8 inch) round layer cake**

*For the sponge*

275g (10oz) salted butter, softened

275g (10oz) light muscovado sugar

5 medium eggs, beaten (weigh the eggs to ensure you have the same weight as the butter, sugar and flour: 275g/10oz)

275g (10oz) self-raising flour

3 tsp vanilla extract

70–100ml (3–3½fl oz) milk

*For the buttercream*

250g (9oz) unsalted butter

500g (1lb 2oz) golden icing sugar

1 quantity of Salted Caramel (see page 80), cooled

*For the decoration*

1 quantity of Salted Caramel (see page 80), warmed

100g (3½oz) toffee popcorn

**TOP TIP**

Ensure the buttercreamed cake is properly chilled before adding the salted caramel drip.

**TO MAKE THE SPONGES**

1   Preheat the oven to 165°C fan (185°C/355°F/Gas 4). Grease and line the base and sides of three 20cm (8-inch) round shallow cake tins.

2   Follow the instructions on page 80 to make the sponge batter and spoon evenly into the 3 tins. Bake for 25 minutes until risen and golden brown.

3   Remove from the oven and cool in the tin for 10 minutes before turning out and leaving to cool on a wire rack. Wrap the layer cakes with cling film and chill before filling.

**TO MAKE THE BUTTERCREAM**

1   Combine the ingredients in a large mixing bowl and beat until smooth.

**TO ASSEMBLE THE CAKE**

1   Remove the cakes from the fridge and place the base layer on a cake plate. Spread with buttercream and place the next layer on top. Spread with more buttercream and add the final layer. Spread a generous layer of buttercream over the top and sides of the cake and neaten with a side scraper and palette knife for the top. Chill the cake until firm.

2   Warm the salted caramel so it flows and is fairly runny. Pour it into a small disposible piping bag and snip off the end. Pipe a drizzle of salted caramel around the outer edge of the cake to encourage the drips down the side of the cake. Fill the top of the cake with the remainder of the caramel and use a small cranked handle palette knife to spread the caramel across the surface.

2   Pile the toffee popcorn over the top and down one side of the cake to decorate.

This cake can be kept for up to 3 days, serve at room temperature. It can be frozen without the popcorn in a suitable container.

# RASPBERRY AND WHITE CHOCOLATE MERINGUE TOWERS

*Question: what could be more delicious than a pillowy meringue filled with fresh whipped Chantilly cream, fresh raspberries and white chocolate? Answer: TWO meringues! Your wish is my command – these floating on air, oh-so-light but oh-so-decadent meringues are sandwiched and decorated with the wonderfully sumptuous combination of cream, chocolate and berries. If that doesn't win you friends and influence people…*

**Makes 9 large or 12 smaller towers**

*For the meringues*

5 large egg whites

pinch of salt

300g (11oz) white caster sugar

2 tsp cornflour

1 tsp lemon juice

*For the filling*

300ml (10fl oz) double cream

75g (3oz) caster sugar

2 tsp vanilla bean paste

*For the decoration*

300g (11oz) raspberries

50g (2oz) grated white chocolate

10g (¼oz) freeze-dried raspberries

## TO MAKE THE MERINGUES

1   Preheat the oven to 140°C fan (160°C/325°F/Gas 3). Line 2 large baking sheets with non-stick baking paper.

2   Draw circles 6cm (2½ inches) and 8cm (3¼ inches) in diameter, spaced apart on the underside of the paper.

3   In a super clean bowl, whisk the egg whites with a pinch of salt until stiff peaks form.

4   Whisk in the sugar one tablespoon at a time until glossy and thick. Don't be tempted to rush this stage otherwise the meringue will be gritty and frothy rather than smooth and velvety.

5   Add the cornflour followed by the lemon juice and continue to whisk for 10 minutes.

6   Spoon into the drawn circles on the baking paper, shape an indent on top with the back of a spoon and bake for 1 hour.

7   Turn the oven off and leave the meringues to cool and dry in the oven overnight.

## TO MAKE THE FILLING

1   When you are ready to stack the meringues, whip the cream with the caster sugar and vanilla bean paste in a large bowl until the cream just holds its shape.

## TO ASSEMBLE THE MERINGUE TOWERS

1   Spoon a generous dessertspoon of the sweetened cream onto each of the larger meringues and dress with the raspberries, white chocolate shavings and a sprinkle of freeze-dried raspberries.

2   Stack the slightly smaller meringues on top, repeat with the decoration and serve.

The towers are best eaten on the day they are made. Not suitable for freezing.

### TOP TIP

These meringues need to be made in advance. They will keep well in an airtight container for up to 3 days, allowing you to plan ahead. Make these even smaller for the perfect canape treat.

# RASPBERRY AND PISTACHIO MERINGUE ROULADE

*Surely this has to be one of the most impressive showstoppers – seemingly defying gravity! You'll be surprised how silky smooth yet light as air this meringue tastes – it bakes and handles beautifully so that you can impress your family and friends with your star baker genius. Change the flavours to suit your mood – a cheeky peach purée with passion fruit or a sexy blackcurrant compote with a dash of Cassis.*

**Serves 6–8**

*For the meringue roulade*

4 large egg whites

200g (7oz) caster sugar

1 tsp cornflour

1 tsp lemon juice

icing sugar, to dust

*For the filling*

300ml (10fl oz) double cream

2 tbsp icing sugar

2 tsp vanilla bean paste

200g (7oz) fresh raspberries

25g (1oz) roasted pistachios, chopped

*For the drizzle*

80g (3¼oz) raspberries

2 tbsp icing sugar

½ tsp rose water

### TOP TIPS

___ Remember to have your egg whites at room temperature
___ Don't rush the whisking – the more patience you have with your meringue, the better the result
___ Make sure the bowl is scrupulously clean before whisking the egg whites
___ When it comes to rolling the roulade, show it who's boss, treat it with respect – be firm but fair!

## TO MAKE THE MERINGUE ROULADE

1   Preheat oven to 140°C fan (160°C/325°F/Gas 3). Line a 33 x 23cm (13 x 9-inch) roulade tin with non-stick baking paper so it comes up at least 2cm (¾ inch) above the side of the tin

2   In a large, clean bowl, whisk the egg whites until stiff. Add the sugar a teaspoon at a time. Once the sugar is added, add the cornflour followed by the lemon juice and continue mixing for a full 5 minutes.

3   Spoon the meringue into the prepared tin and level. Bake for 25 minutes. Remove and leave to cool in the tin for 5 minutes.

4   Turn out onto a sheet of baking paper dusted with icing sugar set on a wire rack but do not remove the baking paper. Leave to cool.

## TO MAKE THE FILLING AND ASSEMBLE THE ROULADE

1   When you are ready to fill, lightly whip the cream in a large bowl with the icing sugar and vanilla bean paste.

2   Remove the paper from the back of the meringue. Spread the cream over the meringue and sprinkle with fresh raspberries and pistachios. Roll up from the short side using the paper and lift onto a serving plate.

## TO MAKE THE DRIZZLE AND FINISH

1   Crush the raspberries with the sugar and pass through a fine sieve. Add the rose water to the purée to taste.

2   Dust the roulade with icing sugar and then drizzle over the berry drizzle. Serve immediately.

This cake is best eaten on the day it is made and is not suitable for freezing.

# CLASSIC CHOCOLATE ÉCLAIRS

*With so many fans of the chocolate-topped choux cream buns, I wanted to include a recipe to give you the confidence to make them at home. My éclairs are quite rustic, heavy on the cream and chocolate and make a delectable treat. Best eaten on the day they are made, they can also be frozen ready for your next celebration.*

**Makes 8–12 éclairs**

*For the choux pastry*
100g (3½oz) unsalted butter
300ml (10fl oz) water
2 tbsp caster sugar
150g (5oz) plain flour
pinch of salt
4 medium eggs, beaten

*For the chocolate sauce*
250g (9oz) dark chocolate (70% cocoa
  solids), broken into squares
160ml (5½fl oz) double cream
2 tbsp golden syrup
40g (1½oz) unsalted butter

*For the cream filling*
600ml (1 pint) double cream, lightly
  whipped until it just holds its shape

**TO MAKE THE CHOUX PASTRY**

1 Melt the butter with the water and sugar in a heavy-based pan over a medium heat. Bring to the boil and then turn off the heat and immediately add the flour and salt.

2 Beat thoroughly and vigorously with a wooden spoon until the mixture forms a small ball that comes away cleanly from the pan.

3 Transfer the dough to a bowl of a stand mixer. Leave to cool for 10 minutes and then gradually beat in the beaten egg a little at a time until fully incorporated and glossy.

4 Preheat the oven to 180°C fan (200°C/400°F/Gas 6) and sprinkle a non-stick baking tray with cold water (this will encourage steam when the choux are in the oven for maximum lift).

5 Fit a large piping bag with a plain nozzle and spoon in the choux batter. Pipe generous lines about 10cm (4 inches) in length well spaced apart on the baking tray. Flatten any points with a finger dampened in cold water.

6 Bake for 10 minutes and then increase the temperature to 200°C fan (220°C/425°F/Gas 7) for a further 15 minutes until golden and brown. Remove the choux and turn off the oven.

7 Pierce each bun with a bamboo skewer or knife to allow the steam to escape. Return to the oven for 10 minutes to continue drying and then transfer to a wire rack to cool.

**TO MAKE THE CHOCOLATE SAUCE**

1 Place all the ingredients in heavy-based saucepan and gently heat until fully combined. Transfer to a large pouring jug to cool.

**TO ASSEMBLE THE ÉCLAIRS**

1 Slice each éclair in half lengthways. Spoon the freshly whipped cream into a piping bag fitted with a plain or star nozzle and fill the éclairs with cream. Spoon the warm chocolate sauce over each of the pastries and leave to set.

# PROFITEROLE TOWER

*This impressive tower of chilled profiteroles will take centre stage at a dinner party. The choux are filled and stacked with fresh cream. They ooze decadence as the warm chocolate sauce is poured over at the last minute for maximum effect, it guarantees a round of applause.*

**Makes 24–30 profiteroles**

*For the profiteroles*

1 quantity of Choux Pastry
   (see page 88)

1 quantity of Cream Filling
   (see page 88)

1 quantity of Chocolate Sauce
   (see page 88)

**TOP TIP**

The profiteroles and éclairs (see page 88) can be frozen after filling with cream in a suitable container. Defrost in the fridge and then continue with the chocolate sauce.

## TO MAKE THE PROFITEROLES

1   Make the choux pastry following the instructions following the instructions on page 88.
2   Preheat the oven to 180°C fan (200°C/400°F/Gas 6) and sprinkle a non-stick baking tray with cold water.
3   Fit a large piping bag with a plain nozzle and spoon in the choux batter. Pipe small rounds well spaced apart onto the baking tray. Flatten any points with a finger dampened in cold water.
4   Bake for 10 minutes and then increase the temperature to 200°C fan (220°C/425°F/Gas 7) for a further 15 mintues until golden and brown. Remove the choux and turn off the oven.
5   Pierce each bun with a bamboo skewer or knife to allow the steam to escape. Return to the oven for 10 minutes to continue drying then transfer to a wire rack to cool.

## TO ASSEMBLE THE PROFITEROLE TOWER

1   Fill a piping bag with the freshly whipped cream. Snip the end off and then insert the tip into the profiterole to inject cream to fill. Repeat with all the profiteroles. Use additional cream (or a little chocolate sauce) to help hold the profiteroles in place as you stack these on a large serving stand (one with a lip is recommended).
2   Chill the buns at this stage if you intend to serve the tower at the table with all the theatre!
3   Warm the chocolate sauce in a microwave or over a pan of simmering water until it is runny and fluid and then carefully pour over the profiterole tower from the top – turning the stand as you work to ensure all the profiteroles are drizzled with chocolate.

Serve immediately. The profiteroles are best eaten on the day they are made.

# RHUBARB AND CUSTARD MINI PAVLOVAS

*There's something quintessentially charming about meringue – from the classic Eton mess of fresh strawberries, whipped cream and crushed meringue to the impressive pavlova piled high with cream and summer berries. Once you have mastered making a pavlova – you can experiment with the fillings. I have chosen a modern interpretation of the classic combination of rhubarb and custard for these mini pavlovas.*

**Makes 15–18 mini pavlova**

*For the meringues*
5 large egg whites
pinch of salt
300g (11oz) caster sugar
2 tsp cornflour
1 tsp lemon juice

*For the rhubarb*
400g (14oz) fresh rhubarb,
    cut into 3cm (1¼-inch) batons
100g (3½oz) caster sugar
100ml (3½fl oz) water
2 tsp vanilla bean paste

*For the custard*
1 vanilla pod
250ml (8fl oz) whole milk
3 medium egg yolks
145g (4½oz) caster sugar
40g (1½oz) plain flour
400ml (14fl oz) double cream

## TO MAKE THE MERINGUES

1   Preheat the oven to 140°C fan (160°C/325°F/Gas 3).
2   Draw 9cm (3½-inch) circles, spaced apart, on the underside of some sheets of non-stick baking paper. Place the sheets on a baking tray.
3   In a super clean bowl, whisk the egg whites with a pinch of salt until stiff peaks form. Whisk in the sugar one tablespoon at a time until glossy and thick. Don't be tempted to rush this stage otherwise the meringue will be gritty and frothy rather than smooth and velvety. Add the cornflour followed by the lemon juice and continue to whisk for a full 10 minutes.
4   Spoon into the circles and shape an indent on top of each one with the back of a spoon.
5   Bake for 1 hour. Turn the oven off and leave the meringues to cool and dry in the oven overnight.

## TO MAKE THE RHUBARB

1   Place the rhubarb, sugar, water and vanilla bean paste in a saucepan and simmer gently for about 5–10 minutes until just soft.
2   Remove the rhubarb with a slotted spoon and dry on a paper towel.
3   Return the pan to the heat and keep simmering to reduce the remaining liquid to a thick syrup.
4   Purée half of the fruit with the syrup and then strain through a sieve. Transfer to a clean bowl and refrigerate until needed.

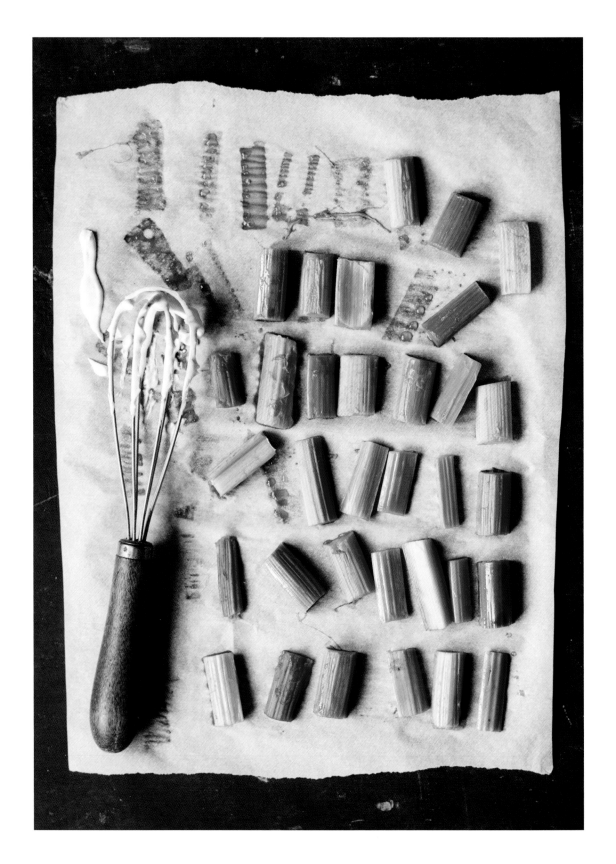

LOAF CAKES, TRAYBAKES AND MERINGUES

### TO MAKE THE CUSTARD

1 Slice the vanilla pod open lengthways and scrape out the seeds. Place the seeds and the pod in a heavy-based saucepan with the milk and bring slowly up to the boil.

2 Meanwhile, blend the egg yolks and 65g (2½oz) of the sugar in a bowl and then sieve in the flour and mix to a thick paste. Pour the just-boiling milk over the egg mixture, whisking constantly for about a minute. Return the mixture to the pan to the heat and bring to the boil, continuously whisking. Boil for a further 2 minutes.

3 Pass the custard through a fine sieve into a clean bowl, and place a sheet of cling film on the surface of the custard to prevent a skin forming. Leave to cool and then refrigerate.

4 When you are ready to fill the pavlovas, whip the cream with the remaining sugar until softly whipped and then fold into the chilled custard.

### TO ASSEMBLE THE MINI PAVLOVAS

1 Place a generous spoonful of custard cream onto each mini pavlova and top with a teaspoon of rhubarb purée. Dress with the reserved steeped rhubarb batons and serve.

These pavlovas are best eaten on the day they are made and are not suitable for freezing. Keep refrigerated until serving.

# CHERRY, STRAWBERRY AND POMEGRANATE PAVLOVA

*My lords, ladies and gentleman, stand aside and make way for our social showstopper: a fresh cherry and pomegranate (with the obligatory strawberry) pavlova. Go big, go for broke, serve in hefty wedges and soak up the summer.*

**Makes 1 x 25cm (10 inch) large pavlova**

*For the meringue*
5 large egg whites
pinch of salt
300g (11oz) caster sugar
2 tsp cornflour
1 tsp lemon juice

*For the topping*
600ml (1 pint) double cream
4 tbsp icing sugar
1 tbsp vanilla bean paste
150g (5oz) cherries
300g (11oz) strawberries, hulled and
    cut into 6 pieces lengthways
75g (3oz) pomegranate seeds

## TO MAKE THE MERINGUE

1  Preheat the oven to 120°C fan (140°C/275°F/Gas 1).
2  Draw a 25cm (10-inch) circle on the underside of a sheet of non-stick baking paper. Place the paper on a baking tray.
3  Make the meringue mixture following the instructions on page 92. Pile the mixture high onto the baking paper sitting inside the drawn circle and shape an indent in the middle with the back of a spoon.
4  Bake for 2½ hours. Turn the oven off and leave the meringue to cool and dry in the oven overnight.

## TO ASSEMBLE THE PAVOLVA

1  Whip the cream together with the sugar and vanilla bean paste until just holding its shape. Fold a third of the cherries and strawberries into the cream.
2  Place the pavlova on a large serving plate or stand. Spoon the cream on top of the pavlova.
3  Pile high with the remaining deliciously fresh cherries, strawberries and pomegranate seeds.

This pavlova is best eaten on the day it is made and is not suitable for freezing. Keep refrigerated until serving.

### TOP TIP

Substitute the fruits for a seasonal twist. Include cranberries, clementines and toasted pistachios at Christmas. Add 100g roasted chopped nuts to the pavlova before baking for extra flavour.

# COFFEE TRAYBAKE

*This all-time classic has certainly enjoyed its reputation as one of the nation's favourites – it still delivers the most wonderful combination of flavours, textures, smells and colours. For the everyday version I have chosen to make a simple traybake – thick squares of coffee sponge cake with a creamy coffee frosting topped with roasted chopped walnuts, chocolate-covered coffee beans and a dusting of cocoa.*

**Serves 16**

*For the sponge*

225g (8oz) unsalted butter

225g (8oz) light muscovado sugar

275g (10oz) self-raising flour

2 level tsp baking powder

4 large eggs, beaten (weigh the eggs
   to ensure you have the same weight
   as the butter and sugar: 220g/8oz),
   beaten

2 shots of espresso topped up to
   100ml (3½fl oz) with full-fat milk

100g (3½oz) chopped walnuts

2 tsp vanilla extract

*For the coffee frosting*

100g (3½oz) unsalted butter

225g (8oz) golden icing sugar

1 tbsp whole milk

1 small shot of espresso, cooled or
   1 heaped tsp of expresso powder
   dissolved in 2 tbsp water

2 tsp vanilla extract

*For the decoration*

100g (3½oz) roasted walnuts, chopped

40g (1½oz) chocolate coffee beans

cocoa powder, for dusting

### TO MAKE THE SPONGE

1   Preheat oven to 160°C fan (180°C/350°F/Gas 4). Grease and line the base and sides of a 30 x 20cm (12 x 8 inch) rectangular cake tin.
2   Measure all the cake ingredients into a large bowl and beat until well blended. Turn the mixture into the prepared tin and level the top.
3   Bake for 35 minutes or until the cake is golden brown, springs back when pressed in the centre with your fingertips and a skewer inserted comes out clean.
4   Remove from the oven. Leave the traybake to cool in the tin. Wrap in cling film and chill before decorating.

### TO MAKE THE COFFEE FROSTING

1   Beat all the ingredients together in a large bowl until smooth.

### TO ASSEMBLE THE TRAYBAKE

1   Spread the frosting evenly and rustically over the cooled cake using a palette knife. Sprinkle with chopped roasted walnuts and coffee beans and dust with a little cocoa powder. Cut into generous squares and serve at room temperature.

The traybake will keep for up to 3 days in a suitable container at room temperature. Suitable for freezing.

### TOP TIP

If you don't have an espresso machine, blend instant coffee granules. Mix 2 level teaspoons with 2 tablespoons of water per 'shot' or use 2 teaspoons espresso powder.

# COFFEE LAYER CAKE

*To transform this cake into a showstopper, I've made two thicker layers of cake and ramped up the decoration to expand your hand-finishing skills. I wanted to modernise the cake, while still keeping a nod to tradition. Suffice to say, there was not a morsel left at the end of the photography shoot.*

**Serves 12**

*For the cake*

1 quantity of Coffee Cake batter
(see page 98)

2 quantities of Coffee Frosting
(see page 98)

*For the decoration*

100g (3½oz) roasted walnuts, chopped

40g (1½oz) chocolate coffee beans

cocoa powder, for dusting

**TO MAKE THE CAKE**

1   Preheat oven to 160°C fan (180°C/350°F/Gas 4). Grease and line the base and sides of two 20cm (8-inch) round, deep sandwich tins.

2   Make the sponge batter following the instructions on page 98 and divide evenly between the prepared cake tins.

3   Bake for 30 minutes or until the cake is golden brown, springs back when pressed in the centre with your fingertips and a skewer inserted comes out clean.

4   Remove from the oven. Turn the cakes out after 5 minutes and leave to cool on a wire rack. Wrap in cling film and chill before decorating.

**TO ASSEMBLE THE CAKE**

1   Place the chilled base layer on a cake plate, stand or board. Spread with a generous layer of coffee frosting and place the second layer on top.

2   Spread the top and sides with frosting and smooth with a palette knife or icing scraper. Chill the cake until firm to the touch.

3   Fit a large piping bag with a fluted nozzle and fill with the remaining coffee frosting. Pipe a series of shells around the base of the cake and repeat around the top outer edge of the cake.

4   Fill the centre of the cake with chopped, roasted walnuts and chocolate coffee beans. Dust the shells with a little cocoa. Cut into wedges and serve at room temperature.

The cake will keep for up to 3 days in a suitable container at room temperature. Suitable for freezing

# LAYER CAKES

# VANILLA LAYER CAKE WITH FRESH STRAWBERRIES

*This vanilla cake is made using the whisking method – using eggs, sugar and flour with no fat. It will be wonderfully light and aerated and is best enjoyed on the day it is made. For this everyday version, simply sandwich two layers with strawberry jam and fresh strawberries.*

**Serves 8**

*For the sponges*

4 medium eggs

125g (4oz) golden caster sugar

1 tsp vanilla bean paste

125g (4oz) plain flour, sifted

*For the filling*

225g (8oz) strawberry jam

250g (9oz) fresh strawberries

icing sugar, to dust

**TO MAKE THE SPONGES**

1  Preheat the oven to 160°C fan (180°C/350°F/Gas 4). Grease and line the base and sides of two 20cm (8-inch) round sandwich tins with non-stick baking paper.

2  In a large heatproof bowl, whisk the eggs with the caster sugar and the vanilla bean paste over a pan of barely simmering water just until the sugar dissolves and reaches a temperature of 40-45°C (104–113°F). Check with a thermometer or your fingers – it should feel like a hot bath.

3  Remove from the heat and transfer to a stand mixer. Continue to whisk at maximum speed for 15 minutes until the batter cools, thickens and triples in size.

4  Add the flour 2 tablespoons at a time and gently fold in with a metal spoon or rubber spatula until fully combined. This will help to avoid lumps without overworking the sponge.

5  Divide the batter between the prepared tins (I do this by weighing each tin as I fill it) and bake in the oven for 25 minutes until the sponges are golden brown and spring back when pressed.

6  Transfer to a wire cooling rack. Leave the cakes to cool for 5 minutes and then turn out and leave to cool completely.

**TO ASSEMBLE THE CAKE**

1  Place the base on a cake plate and spread with the strawberry jam.

2  Slice the fresh strawberries over the top and top with the remaining sponge. Dust with icing sugar.

This cake is best eaten on the day it is made.

# VANILLA LAYER CAKE WITH CHANTILLY CREAM AND SUMMER BERRY COMPOTE

*For a more decadent showstopper, I have chosen to create an impressive triple-layer cake, sandwiched with a silky Chantilly cream and summer berry compote. Brushing the sponges with a fruit syrup also ensures the cake is really fruity and moist.*

**Serves 8–12**

*For the sponges*
6 medium eggs
190g (6½oz) golden caster sugar
2 tsp vanilla bean paste
190g (6½oz) plain flour, sifted

*For the compote*
600g (1lb 5oz) mixed fresh or frozen
    seasonal berries
grated zest of 1 orange and juice
    of ½ orange
golden caster sugar, to taste

*For the Chantilly cream*
600ml (1 pint) double cream
50g (2oz) icing sugar
1 tbsp vanilla bean paste

### TO MAKE THE SPONGES
1   Use the ingredients to make the sponge layers following the instructions on page 105 and using three 20cm (8-inch) cake tins.

### TO MAKE THE COMPOTE
1   Set aside 200g (7oz) of the berries and then gently simmer the remaining berries with the orange zest and juice and sugar in a medium pan. Cool and then drain, reserving 4 tablespoons of the juice.
2   Add 2 tablespoons back to the fruit and use the remaining juice to brush the underside of each sponge. This can be made a day in advance and stored, covered, in the refrigerator.

### TO MAKE THE CHANTILLY CREAM
1   Gently whip together all the ingredients for the filling until the cream just holds its shape.

### TO ASSEMBLE THE CAKE
1   Place the first sponge brushed with the fruit syrup onto a cake plate or stand (juice side up), spread with the whipped cream filling and half the fruit compote. Repeat with the second layer and finish with the top layer (juice side down).
2   Spread with the remaining whipped cream and dress with the reserved fresh berries.

The cake is best eaten on the day it is made. Not suitable for freezing. Keep refrigerated.

### TOP TIP

To add more flavour to the cake, add the zest of 1 orange or lemon before adding the flour. Replace the fruit compote with your favourite jam for a more classic, simple showstopper!

# CHOCOLATE AND SALTED CARAMEL CAKE

*A simple yet delicious chocolate sponge layered with indulgent salted caramel and chocolate buttercream. This chocolate cake is perfect for every day – quick to make and decorate; delicious to eat. I use dark chocolate so the flavour is rich and indulgent. The Swiss meringue buttercream has less sugar than regular buttercream so the cake is wonderfully chocolatey. I have chosen a decoration on the top with crunchy, crispy chocolate-covered malt balls, but you could use homemade truffles.*

**Serves 8–12**

*For the sponges*

250g (9oz) unsalted butter, at room temperature

150g (5oz) golden caster sugar

100g (5oz) light brown sugar

4 large eggs, beaten
(weigh the eggs to ensure you have the same weight as the butter: 250g/9oz)

200g (7oz) self-raising flour

1 tsp baking powder

50g (2oz) cocoa powder

40ml (1½fl oz) whole milk

*For the Swiss meringue buttercream*

115ml (3¾fl oz) egg whites

200g (7oz) golden caster sugar

250g (9oz) unsalted butter, chilled but removed from the fridge 30 minutes before using and cubed

1 tbsp vanilla extract

200g (7oz) dark chocolate
(70% cocoa solids), melted

200g (7oz) Salted Caramel
(see page 80)

*For the decoration*

30g (1¼oz) chocolate malt balls

## TO MAKE THE SPONGES

1 Preheat the oven to 170°C fan (190°C/375°F/Gas 5). Grease and line the base and sides of two 20cm (8-inch) round cake tins.

2 Place the butter and sugars in a large bowl and beat together until light and fluffy. Add the beaten eggs a little at a time until fully incorporated. Sift the flour, baking powder and cocoa together and fold into the cake mixture. Stir in the milk.

3 Divide the batter equally between the prepared tins and level the surface with the back of a spoon. Bake for 20 minutes until the cakes are baked, beginning to shrink away from the sides of the tins and spring back when pressed gently.

4 Remove from the oven and transfer to a wire rack. Leave the cakes to cool in the tins for 5 minutes before turning out to cool completely.

## TO MAKE THE SWISS MERINGUE BUTTERCREAM

1 Place the egg whites, and sugar in a large, clean heatproof bowl and place over a pan of gently simmering water. Whisk with a hand balloon whisk and monitor the temperature until it reaches 61–70°C (142–158°F). This will take about 10 minutes.

2 Remove from the heat and attach to a stand mixer fitted with the whisk attachment. Whisk the meringue until it has thickened, tripled in size and cooled to room temperature. Change the attachment for the beater and add the butter in small batches until fully incorporated and thickened. Whisk in the vanilla extract. Pour in the melted chocolate and salted caramel and mix until combined and smooth.

## TO ASSEMBLE THE CAKE

1 Place one sponge layer on a cake stand. Spread generously with the buttercream and top with the second layer. Spoon the remaining buttercream on top and smooth with a palette knife. Sprinkle with the chocolate malt balls and serve.

This cake will keep at room temperature for 3-5 days. Suitable for freezing if stored in a suitable container with a lid.

# THE ALTHORP CHOCOLATE AND SALTED CARAMEL LAYER CAKE

*I had the pleasure of being invited to Althorp – the ancestral home of Princess Diana – to appear at the Althorp Food and Drink Festival. As a dinner guest of Earl Spencer, I created and presented this cake as a gift to my host. With my enormous thanks to Earl Spencer, Lady Karen Spencer and the entire team at Althorp for such wonderful hospitality, I am delighted to include the recipe, known as The Althorp Layer Cake.*

**Serves 16–20**

*For the sponges*

750g (1lb 11oz) unsalted butter, at room temperature

400g (14oz) golden caster sugar

350g (12oz) light brown sugar

12 large eggs, beaten (weigh the eggs to ensure you have the same weight as the butter: 750g/1lb 11oz)

650g (1lb 7oz) self-raising flour

1 tbsp baking powder

100g (3½oz) cocoa powder

200ml (7fl oz) whole milk

*For the Swiss meringue buttercream*

225ml (8fl oz) egg whites

400g (14oz) golden caster sugar

500g (1lb 2oz) unsalted butter, chilled but removed from the fridge 30 minutes before using, cubed

1 tbsp vanilla extract

500g (1lb 2oz) Salted Caramel (see page 80)

*For the chocolate ganache*

100ml (3½fl oz) double cream

400g (14oz) dark chocolate (70% cocoa solids), broken into pieces

200g (7oz) unsalted butter, cubed

*For the toasted almond praline*

150g (5oz) flaked almonds

250g (9oz) caster sugar

## TO MAKE THE SPONGES

1   Preheat the oven to 170°C fan (190°C/375°F/Gas 5). Grease and line the base and sides of four 25cm (10-inch) round sandwich cake tins (or if you only have 2 tins, make it in 2 batches).

2   Place the butter and sugars in a large bowl and beat together until light and fluffy. Add the beaten eggs a little at a time until fully incorporated. Sift the flour, baking powder and cocoa together and fold into the cake mixture. Stir in the milk.

3   Divide the batter equally between the prepared tins and level the surface with the back of a spoon. Bake for 30 minutes until the cakes are baked, beginning to shrink away from the sides of the tins and spring back when pressed gently.

4   Remove from the oven and transfer to a wire rack. Leave the cakes to cool in the tins for 5 minutes before turning out to cool completely. Wrap gently in cling film and place in the fridge to chill before filling.

## TO MAKE THE SWISS MERINGUE BUTTERCREAM

1   Place the egg whites and sugar in a large, clean heatproof bowl and place over a pan of gently simmering water. Whisk with a hand balloon whisk and monitor the temperature until it reaches 61–70°C (142–158°F). This will take about 10 minutes.

2   Remove from the heat and transfer to a stand mixer fitted with the whisk attachment. Whisk the meringue until it has thickened, tripled in size and cooled to room temperature. Change the whisk attachment for the beater and add the butter in small batches until fully incorporated and thickened. Whisk in the vanilla extract.

3   Remove the bowl from the mixer and fold in half of the salted caramel (reserve the rest for building the cake) until combined and smooth.

### TO MAKE THE CHOCOLATE GANACHE

1  Place the cream in a small saucepan and bring to the boil.
2  Meanwhile, place the broken chocolate pieces and cubed butter together in a large heatproof bowl and gently microwave on high for 1-2 minutes to gently soften and begin to melt.
3  Remove the cream when it is at a rolling boil and pour immediately over the chocolate and butter.
4  Stir with a rubber spatula until completely melted and smooth. Transfer to a bowl or plastic container and leave to cool.
5  Spoon 3 generous tablespoons of the salted caramel Swiss meringue buttercream into a bowl and stir in 3 tablespoons of the chocolate ganache to create a rich, silky-smooth buttercream. Set aside.

### TO MAKE THE TOASTED ALMOND PRALINE

1  Preheat the oven to 170°C fan (190°C/375°F/Gas 5). Lay the flaked almonds on a sheet of non-stick baking paper on a baking tray and bake for 10-15 minutes, turning occasionally until golden and toasted. Remove from the oven and leave to cool slightly.
2  Place the sugar in a large, heavy-based non-stick frying pan over a medium heat without stirring, until the sugar has all melted. Continue to heat until the sugar turns to a golden caramel colour. Tip the almonds into the caramel. Swirl around to cover and then transfer the praline onto a baking tray lined with non-stick baking paper to cool and harden.
3  Crack the praline into pieces with a sharp cook's knife or blunt rolling pin. Reserve at least 12 larger pieces for decoration and finely chop the remainder into smaller pieces.

### TO ASSEMBLE THE CAKE

1  Place the first chilled cake on a 10" cake board.
2  Spread with salted caramel Swiss meringue buttercream and make a well in the centre around 15cm (6 inches) in diameter. Pour in half the remaining salted caramel and level with the palette knife.
3  Place the next cake directly on top. Sprinkle generously with bite-sized pieces of almond praline.
4  Add the next cake and repeat with salted caramel Swiss meringue buttercream and a pool of the last of the salted caramel.
5  Add the final layer of cake. Chill at this stage for 10-15 minutes to firm the cake so that it is easier to handle.
6  Spread a thin layer of salted caramel buttercream over the sides and top of the cake to create a crumb coat. Place in the fridge for up to 1 hour to chill completely.

'Mich is the best baker of cakes that I've ever come across, anywhere on the Planet. Sensational tastes, beautiful designs and all carried off with unique charm and delicious humour.'
Charles Spencer,
9th Earl Spencer

7  Apply a second generous layer (3–5mm/ ⅛ inch) of buttercream over the sides and top of the cake to cover the cake and base board. Use a side scraper to create smooth, straight sides and a flat top.

8  Place the cake in the fridge for about 30–60 minutes to firm. Blend the remaining buttercream with a similar quantity of ganache to create a chocolate ganache salted caramel buttercream. Place in a piping bag fitted with a teardrop No. 124 nozzle.

9  Place the chilled cake on a wire rack. Place the remaining chocolate ganache in a jug and heat either in the microwave or in a heatproof bowl placed over a pan of simmering water until fluid and warm, but not overly runny.

10  Pour the ganache onto the top of the cake and gently smooth out with a pallet knife to cover the top and sides of the cake until completely covered. Leave to set for a few minutes.

11  Carefully lift and remove the cake from the wire rack, neaten the base of the cake with a small, sharp knife. Place the cake on an upturned bowl and gently cup handfuls of blitzed praline around the base of the cake to decorate. Leave to set before transferring to a generous, impressive cake stand or plate.

12  Hand pipe 12 swizzles of buttercream evenly around the top edge of the cake and decorate each with a large shard of the reserved almond praline.

This cake will keep at room temperature for 3–5 days. Store in a cake box if necessary.

# LEMON AND ELDERFLOWER LAYER CAKE

*As soon as it was announced that the wedding cake for TRH The Duke and Duchess of Sussex would be a luscious lemon and elderflower cake – with elderflower Swiss meringue buttercream, simply dressed with fresh white peonies – it has catapulted to the top of the most desirable flavours and style of wedding cake. It makes perfect sense for me to include a single-tier version that can be dressed with a cornucopia of fresh frosted fruits. After all, if it's good enough for The Royals…*

**Makes 1 x 20cm (8 inch) layer cake**

*For the sponges*

260g (9½oz) self-raising flour

1 tbsp baking powder

pinch of salt

160ml (5½fl oz) milk

80ml (3fl oz) freshly
   squeezed lemon juice

240g (8½oz) unsalted butter

grated zest of 2 lemons

400g (14oz) golden caster sugar

4 large eggs, beaten

2 tsp vanilla bean paste

*For the lemon curd*

juice and zest of 2 lemons

2 medium eggs, beaten

175g (6oz) golden caster sugar

50g (2oz) unsalted butter

*For the Swiss meringue buttercream*

225ml (8fl oz) egg whites

400g (14oz) caster sugar

565g (1¼lb) unsalted butter, chilled

3 tsp vanilla bean paste

4 tbsp elderflower cordial

*For the decoration*

elderflower cordial, for brushing

fresh fruits, cleaned and dried

egg white, whisked to create a froth

caster sugar

pearl lustre spray

## TO MAKE THE SPONGES

1  Preheat oven to 170°C fan (190°C/375°F/Gas 5) and line three 20cm (8-inch) round tins with non-stick baking paper.

2  Mix the flour, baking powder and salt together. In a separate jug, mix the milk and lemon juice together.

3  Place the butter and lemon zest in a stand mixer and beat until smooth. Add the sugar and continue to beat until light and fluffy.

4  Add the beaten egg a little at a time and then add the vanilla.

5  Add the flour and the milk mixture in alternate additions, beginning and ending with the flour.

6  Divide the batter equally between the tins and level the surface.

7  Bake for 25–30 minutes until baked, golden, risen and a skewer inserted in the centre comed out clean. Remove the tins from the oven.

8  Leave to cool in the tins for 10 minutes and then turn out onto a wire rack to cool completely. Wrap in cling film and chill to firm.

## TO MAKE THE LEMON CURD

1  Place all the ingredients in a medium saucepan and heat over a medium–low heat until thickened. Do not let the curd boil.

2  Sieve to remove all the pips and rind, transfer to a glass bowl and cover with cling film (directly in contact with the surface of the curd). Chill for at least 3 hours in the fridge or until ready to use. The curd will keep for 14 days in the fridge.

## TO MAKE THE SWISS MERINGUE BUTTERCREAM

1  Place the egg whites and sugar in a heatproof bowl over a pan of simmering water and whisk with a hand balloon whisk as the mixture heats to a temperature of 65–71°C (149–160°F). Remove from the heat.

2  Transfer the mixture to a stand mixer fitter with the whisk attachment and whisk until the meringue cools and triples in size.

3  Change the attachment to the beater and slowly add the chilled butter. Add the vanilla and elderflower cordial 1 tablespoon at a time and whisk until smooth.

$\longrightarrow$

LAYER CAKES

**TO ASSEMBLE THE CAKE**

1   Place one layer of sponge on a cake stand or cake board and brush with elderflower cordial.

2   Spread a thin layer of buttercream on top, making an extra, thicker ridge around the outside edge. Fill the centre with 3–4 tablespoons lemon curd.

3   Repeat with the next layer and finally lay the third cake on top. Apply a thin crumb coat of buttercream over the top and sides of the cake and chill for about 45–60 minutes until completely firm.

4   Frost the top and sides of the cake with the remaining buttercream. Start with the top and smooth with a palette knife. Allow the frosting to hang over the sides of the cake.

5   Spread the frosting over the sides of the cake and use a side scraper to smooth the icing and create a collar. Chill until firm.

6   Use a pastry brush to brush the clean, dry fruit with the froth of the egg white and then dip the fruit in caster sugar. Leave to dry on a tray.

7   Dress the top of the cake with the frosted fruit and finish with a pearl lustre spray.

Store in the refrigerator for up to 3 days. Suitable for freezing without the fruit.

# LEMON AND ELDERFLOWER TRIPLE-TIER CELEBRATION CAKE

*Expanding this cake to a three-tier showstopper elevates it in every sense of the word. The tiers can be made and chilled (or frozen) ahead of time and assembled in situ. If you would prefer an alternative decoration, dress with fresh fruits or summer berries or delicate edible flowers. This is the perfect summer wedding celebration cake and one of my favourites.*

**Makes 1 x three tier cake**

*For the sponges*

780g (1lb 11½oz) self-raising flour

3 tbsp baking powder

large pinch of salt

720g (1lb 10oz) butter

6 lemons

1.2kg (2lb 11oz) caster sugar

12 large eggs, beaten

6 tbsp vanilla bean paste

480ml (16fl oz) milk

240ml (7½fl oz) lemon juice

*For the lemon curd*

juice and zest of 4 lemons

4 medium eggs, beaten

350g (12oz) golden caster sugar

100g (3½oz) unsalted butter

*For the Swiss meringue buttercream*

450ml (15fl oz) egg whites

800g (1¾lb) caster sugar

1.1kg (2½lb) unsalted butter, chilled

6 tsp vanilla bean paste

8 tbsp elderflower cordial

*For the decoration*

elderflower cordial, for brushing

fresh peonies

6", 8" and 10" cake boards

10 dowelling rods

## TO MAKE THE SPONGES

1   Preheat oven to 170°C fan (190°C/375°F/Gas 5) and line three 15cm (6-inch), three 20cm (8-inch) and three 25cm (10-inch) round cake tins with non-stick baking paper.

2   Follow the instructions for the lemon and elderflower layer cake on page 115 to make the sponge batter.

3   Divide the batter between the tins pouring 210g (7½oz) into each of the 15cm (6-inch) tins, 420g (15oz) into the 20cm (8-inch) tins and 630g (1lb 6oz) into the 25cm (10-inch) tins.

4   Bake the sponges and then cool according to the instructions on page 115.

## TO MAKE THE LEMON CURD

1   Follow the instructions on page 115 to make the lemon curd.

## TO MAKE THE SWISS MERINGUE BUTTERCREAM

1   Follow the instructions on page 115 to make the Swiss meringue buttercream.

## TO ASSEMBLE THE CAKE

1   Assemble the three tiers separately following the instructions on page 117.

2   Insert trimmed dowelling rods into the base two tiers (cut flush with the top of the cake) and stack centrally in position either onto a cake board or cake stand.

3   Dress with beautiful fresh peonies and foliage – remember to tie the stems with floristry tape.

This cake cannot easily be transported once stacked and decorated – it would make sense to assemble this cake in situ.

# STRAWBERRY SHORTCAKE FLORAL STACKS

*This is the perfect solution for non-cake lovers. Buttery vanilla shortcake biscuits that can be flavoured with orange, lemon, rose or lavender, filled and stacked with fresh Chantilly cream and summer berries and decorated with the most fragrant and vibrant edible flowers. Make sure you source your flowers from a reputable, sustainable grower and keep them refrigerated until the very last moment.*

**Makes 12–15 stacks**

*For the shortcake*

200g (7oz) unsalted butter

200g (7oz) golden caster sugar

1 medium egg, beaten

400g (14oz) plain flour, plus extra
   for dusting

1 tsp vanilla bean paste

1 tsp baking powder

grated zest of 2 lemons and 1 orange,
   2 tsp crushed lavender or
   1 tsp rose water (optional)

*For the decoration*

1 litre (1¾ pints) double cream

200g (7oz) caster sugar

1 tbsp vanilla bean paste

300g (11oz) strawberry preserve

sliced strawberries

fresh edible flowers

finely blitzed dried rose petals

## TOP TIP

If you can't find edible flowers, dress the stacks with macarons, redcurrants, hand- piped meringue swirls and toasted flaked almonds.

## TO MAKE THE SHORTCAKE

1   Cream the butter and sugar together in a large bowl and then add the beaten egg to combine. Gently fold in the flour, vanilla, baking powder and zest, lavender or rose water, if using, and mix until a dough forms. Wrap the dough in cling film and chill for 30 minutes.

2   Preheat the oven to 180°C fan (200°C/400°F/Gas 6) and line a baking sheet with non-stick baking paper. Lightly flour a work surface and roll the dough to a thickness of 5mm (¼ inch).

3   Stamp out 6cm (2½-inch) fluted rounds and place on the prepared baking sheet, spaced well apart.

4   Bake for 10–12 minutes or until pale golden. Transfer to a wire rack to cool.

## TO ASSEMBLE THE STACKS

1   When you are ready to fill the stacks, whisk the cream with the sugar and vanilla bean paste until softly whipped and holding its shape. Fit a large piping bag with a plain nozzle and spoon in the cream.

2   Place half the rounds in position and pipe beautiful large pearls of cream around the outer edges of the shortcake. Repeat on the inner edge or centre and then spoon or drizzle a little strawberry preserve between the pearls, keeping it contained on the inside.

3   Place a lid of shortcake carefully on top of each cream-topped round and repeat with another covering of piped cream pearls.

4   Decorate with sliced strawberries, raspberries and fresh edible flowers and finish with a sprinkle of blitzed dried rose leaves.

The undecorated shortcake can be kept in an airtight container for up to 7 days. Filled and decorated, they are best eaten on the day of making– not suitable for freezing.

# TRIPLE-LAYER STRAWBERRY SHORTCAKE NUMERALS

*I love the WOW factor of this cake! It is amazingly impressive, colourful and spectacular. A true showstopper – yet relatively simple to create. It is much less time-consuming than some of the other recipes, but because everything has to be made and prepared fresh, it leaves less time for any errors – not that there will be!*

**Makes a set of double digits**

1 quantity of Strawberry Shortcake
    Floral Stacks dough (see page 121)

*For the filling*
1 litre (1¾ pints) double cream
200g (7oz) caster sugar
1 tbsp vanilla bean paste
300g (11oz) strawberry preserve

*For the decoration*
sliced strawberries and raspberries
fresh edible flowers
finely blitzed dried rose petals

**TO MAKE THE SHORTCAKE**

1   Preheat the oven to 180°C fan (200°C/400°F/Gas 6) and line a baking sheet with non-stick baking paper. Lightly flour a work surface and roll the dough to a thickness of 5mm (¼ inch).

2   Cut out 2 sets of each of your chosen numerals (or letters) and place on the prepared baking sheet, spaced well apart.

3   Bake for 15-18 minutes or until pale golden. Transfer to a wire rack to cool.

**TO MAKE THE FILLING AND ASSEMBLE THE SHORTCAKE**

1   When you are ready to fill the numerals, whisk the cream with the sugar and vanilla until softly whipped and holding its shape. Fit a large piping bag with a plain nozzle and spoon in the cream.

2   Place the base numerals/letters in position and pipe beautiful large pearls of cream around the outer edges of the shortcake. Repeat on the inner edge or centre and then spoon or drizzle a little strawberry preserve between the pearls, keeping it contained on the inside.

3   Place the lid of shortcake carefully on top and repeat with another covering of hand-piped cream pearls.

4   Decorate with sliced strawberries, raspberries and fresh edible flowers and finish with a sprinkle of blitzed dried rose leaves.

The undecorated shortcakes can be kept in an airtight container for up to 7 days. Filled and decorated, they are best eaten on the day they are made – not suitable for freezing.

**TOP TIP**

For a chocoholics option – use the Chocolate Cream (see page 63) and dress with chocolate truffles, chocolate shavings, toffee popcorn, salted chocolate pretzels and drizzle with chocolate ganache or salted caramel.

# RED VELVET CAKE WITH CREAM CHEESE FROSTING

*The red velvet cake enjoys its status as one of the most indulgent, luxurious, impressive and recognisable cakes. It's important the flavour and decoration lives up to the expectation for this everyday bake so I have chosen to layer with fresh cream cheese frosting and finish with a hand-piped design and fresh redcurrants.*

**Serves 12**

*For the sponges*
300g (11oz) plain flour
55g (2oz) cocoa powder
½ tsp salt
150g (5oz) unsalted butter,
    at room temperature
280g (10oz) golden caster sugar
2 large eggs, beaten
1 tsp vanilla extract
250ml (8fl oz) buttermilk
2 tsp red food colouring gel
1 tsp bicarbonate of soda
1 tsp distilled vinegar

*For the cream cheese frosting*
75g (3oz) unsalted butter, chilled
450g (1lb) icing sugar
190g (6½oz) cream cheese
vanilla extract, to taste (optional)

*For the decoration*
redcurrants

## TO MAKE THE SPONGES

1 Preheat the oven to 170°C fan (190°C/375°F/Gas 5). Grease three 20cm (8-inch) sandwich tins and line the bottoms with non-stick baking paper.

2 Sift the flour, cocoa powder and salt together and set aside.

3 In a large bowl, start whisking the butter. Once creamy, incorporate the sugar in two batches, whisking between each addition. Slowly whisk in the beaten eggs and then the vanilla extract.

4 Start adding the flour mixture to the butter mixture in batches, whisking well but slowly after each addition. The cake mixture will be thick. Add the buttermilk and food colouring and whisk until smooth.

5 Working quickly, combine the bicarbonate of soda and vinegar. Fold into the cake mixture. Once incorporated, divide the mixture between the three tins.

6 Bake for 25 minutes, or until a skewer inserted in the centre comes out clean. Remove and cool slightly in the tin before turning out onto a wire rack to cool completely.

7 Trim the cakes so they are level and crumb the offcuts to use as decoration at the end.

## TO MAKE THE CREAM CHEESE FROSTING

1 Prepare the cream cheese frosting following the instructions on page 30.

2 Transfer to a covered bowl or sealed container and chill before using.

$\longrightarrow$

LAYER CAKES

## TO ASSEMBLE THE CAKE

1 Place the base layer of cake on a cake plate, stand or board and spread with one-third of the cream cheese frosting. Repeat with the second layer.
2 Place the top layer on the cake and score into 12 even portions using a sharp knife.
3 Fit a large piping bag with a teardrop nozzle and fill with the remaining cream cheese frosting.
4 Starting at the outer edge of the cake, with the wider end of the teardrop nozzle closest to the cake, pressure pipe from side to side to create a swizzle of frosting as you draw the nozzle towards the centre of the cake. Repeat all around the cake until each scored section is covered.
5 Decorate with little clusters of fresh redcurrants and crumb a little of the red velvet cake offcuts onto the portions.

This cake will keep for up to 3 days but is best eaten on the day it is made. Keep cool.

# RED VELVET CAKE WITH WHITE CHOCOLATE MIRROR-GLAZE

*My son described this as 'a Ferrari in a cake' and who can argue with that? This red mirror glaze is made with white chocolate and glucose syrup to create a super-shiny, vibrant red, glossy mirror glaze. This technique can be used with other colours to personalise your cakes. The secret is to have all the colours at the right temperature and the cake pre-frozen so the icing sets quickly as it is poured.*

**Serves 12**

*For the cake*

1 triple-layer Red Velvet Cake
   (see page 126)
1½ quantities of Cream Cheese
   Frosting (see page 126)

*For the mirror glaze*

20g (¾oz) gelatine powder
270ml (9fl oz) cold water
300g (11oz) granulated sugar
280g (10oz) liquid glucose
200g (7oz) sweetened condensed milk
300g (11oz) white chocolate chips
white food colouring gel
red extra food colouring gel

*For the decoration*

fresh strawberries and redcurrants
white sugar pearls

## TO MAKE THE CAKE

1 Prepare the red velvet sponges following the instructions on page 126 and place on a 20cm (8-inch) cake board. Sandwich and cover the top and sides with the cream cheese frosting and smooth with a palette knife and cake scraper so you have a perfectly straight and flat covered cake.

2 Place in the fridge to firm and then transfer the cake to the freezer for at least 1 hour prior to covering.

## TO MAKE THE MIRROR GLAZE

1 Place the gelatine in a small bowl and pour 120ml (4fl oz) of the cold water over it. Stir and set aside to swell for 10 minutes.

2 Measure the sugar, remaining water and liquid glucose together in a large saucepan and bring to the boil up to a temperature of 103°C (217°F) – you will need a digital thermometer to accurately record this. Remove from the heat and whisk in the gelatine. Once combined, pour in the sweetened condensed milk and whisk until fully combined.

3 Place the white chocolate chips in a large bowl and pour the hot sugar syrup over the chocolate. Leave to sit for 5 minutes without mixing to allow the chocolate to melt. Use a handheld electric blender to blend the glaze so it is fully mixed and smooth.

4 Transfer 4 tablespoons of the glaze into a smaller jug and colour this with white food colouring. Colour the remaining glaze with red extra gel to achieve a rich, intense colour.

5 Monitor the temperature as the glazes cool – each glaze needs to achieve a temperature of 28–30°C (82–86°F) before it can be poured. Too warm and it will run straight off; too cold and it will be too thick and gloopy.

 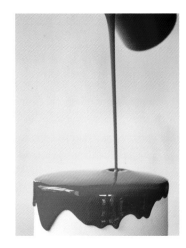 

**TO ASSEMBLE THE CAKE**

1   When you are ready to glaze, remove the cake from the freezer
    and stand it on an upturned bowl place over a shallow baking tray
    lined with cling film.
2   Pour the red glaze in the centre of the cake and keep pouring as
    it covers the top and runs down the sides of the cake.
3   Leave to settle for a few minutes before adding a drizzle of white
    glaze across one corner of the cake – you can afford to be quite bold
    with this as the glaze will merge and continue to slowly run down
    the cake creating a marbling effect.
4   Leave the glaze to settle for 15 minutes. Use a sharp knife to
    remove the drips from the base of the cake and then lift the cake
    carefully onto a presentation cake board.
5   Decorate with a selection of redcurrants, sliced strawberries and
    white sugar pearls. Serve the cake at room temperature.

This cake will keep for up to 3 days stored in the fridge. Serve at room
temperature. Not suitable for freezing.

# CHOCOLATE FONDANT CAKE WITH FRESH ROSES

*Certain occasions call for a more formal cake and there is something charming and quintessential about this simple decorated design made of a chocolate cake finished with fresh garden roses. Covered with soft chocolate fondant, the sophisticated and regal finish is complemented by a length of ribbon around the base.*

**Serves 16–20**

*For the cake*

1 x 20cm (8-inch) cake of your choice layered and covered with flavoured buttercream of your choice

*For the decoration*

1kg (2¼lb) chocolate fondant sugar paste

icing sugar, for dusting

ribbon

a little Royal Icing (see page 199), for fixing

fresh roses

## TO MAKE THE CAKE

1 Cover the cake neatly in buttercream refrigerate until firm. Make sure the cake comes to a depth of 10cm (4 inches) – either by building up the number of layers or adding an extra 20cm (8-inch) cake drum beneath the cake before covering.

2 Remove the cake from the fridge 15 minutes before covering.

## TO DECORATE THE CAKE

1 Knead and roll the chocolate fondant on a clean work surface lightly dusted with icing sugar to a thickness of 3-5mm (⅛ inch).

2 Lift and place the fondant over the prepared cake. Shape and smooth the top and sides and use an icing smoother for a professional finish.

3 Trim around the base of the cake and transfer to a cake plate, stand or board. Fix a length of ribbon around the base, held in place with royal icing.

4 When you are ready to serve, dress with fresh garden roses – make sure to tape up the stems in floristry tape before use.

Will keep for 3–5 days at room temperature. Suitable for freezing. Defrost at room temperature.

# CHOCOLATE CAKE WITH HAND-MOULDED ROSES

*For a more extravagant or special celebration or to expand your hand finishing skills, use the template on page 217, scribed onto the cake and hand piped in a soft golden caramel colour. Make roses from the same chocolate fondant and hand pipe royal iced leaves. These can be sprayed with bronze lustre before dressing the cake.*

**Makes 1 x 20cm (8 inch) cake**

1 x 20cm (8 inch) cake of your choice layered and covered with flavoured buttercream of your choice

*For the decoration*

1kg (2¼lb) chocolate fondant sugar paste

icing sugar, for dusting

ribbon

1 quantity of Royal Icing (see page 199), coloured with caramel food colouring gel

bronze lustre spray

*For the hand-moulded roses*

200g (7oz) chocolate fondant sugar paste

## TOP TIP

Change the colour of the fondant, hand piping, leaves and roses to personalise your cake. Follow the recipe for the chocolate and salted caramel cake on page 109.

**TO MAKE THE CAKE**

1 Prepare the cake, covering with the chocolate fondant sugar paste following the instructions on page 136.

**TO MAKE THE HAND MOULDED ROSES**

1 Knead the chocolate fondant sugar paste on a clean work surface lightly dusted with icing sugar until soft and pliable but not sticky. Roll into a sausage, about 3cm (1¼ inches) diameter. Cut into 4mm (⅛ inch) thick discs using a sharp knife.

2 Discard the end piece, then place 8 discs inside a clear plastic document holder (with the long and base side slit open with a sharp knife or scissors).

3 Press the discs through the plastic to flatten and shape just one side of each petal. Open up the document holder and remove the first petal from the sheet. Turn it over and roll it up tightly to create the centre of the rose. The thinned edge should be at the top and the thicker edge remains at the base.

4 Remove the second and third petals from the sheet and place around the curled central petal. Ensure they are high enough up that once fixed in position can be gently curled and shaped at the top to create the shape and movement.

5 Remove the final 5 petals one at a time and add these around the rose, tucking each one inside the next. Shape the petals as before until the rose is shaped.

6 Use a sharp knife to carefully remove the excess base of the rose. Place on a workboard, spray with bronze lustre and leave to firm. These can be made up to 3 months in advance and stored in a clean cake box.

## TO ASSEMBLE THE CAKE

1   Trace the template on page 217 onto a sheet of tracing paper.
    Position this against the cake and prick through the design onto
    the cake with a scribe.

2   Repeat twice more so you have the design 3 times in total around
    the cake. Fill a piping bag with caramel-coloured royal icing,
    fitted with a No. 3 piping nozzle. Starting at the top, hand pipe the
    design onto the cake, using the template to join the dots.

3   Hand pipe a series of royal-iced leaves onto a sheet of waxed paper
    with a No. 69 nozzle using the same caramel coloured royal icing
    (see page 199).  Leave overnight to firm. Spray with bronze lustre
    and leave to dry. Carefully remove with a small, sharp knife.

4   Fix the roses and leaves onto the top of the cake.

Store and serve at room temperature. Will keep for 3–5 days at
room temperature.

# 'SHERBET PIPS' CROWN CAKES

*Whether you call these pearls, dots, bubbles or pips the technique of hand piping coloured pearls on cakes using different colours and sizes can be an extremely effective decoration – one that can be applied to individual crown cakes, a single-tier celebration cake or a multi-tiered stacked cake. By changing the colours, you can dramatically change the tone of the cake, to perfectly complement many special celebrations.*

**Makes 25 cakes**

*For the cakes*

1 x 25cm (10 inch) square cake
 (I suggest making the fruit cake on
 page 207 but using a 25cm (10 inch)
 square cake tin and baking at 125–
 130°C fan (145–150°C/275–300°F/
 Gas 1–2) for 3 hours)

250g (9oz) apricot jam (allow 10g/½oz
 per cake), boiled

1.8kg (4lb ) marzipan (allow 75g/3oz
 per cake)

brandy or cooled boiled water, for
 brushing

2.5kg (5½lb) fondant sugar paste
 (allow 100g/3½oz per cake)

*For the decoration*

1cm (½-inch) width ribbon for each
 cake (allow 20cm (8 inches) per
 cake)

1 quantity of Royal Icing (see page 199)
 – either white or coloured

pink, yellow and green food colouring
 gels

3mm (⅛-inch) width ribbon for the
 heart picks (allow 20cm (8 inches)
 per cake)

## TO ICE THE CAKES

1   Chill the cake for 2–4 hours (or overnight) to firm and make it easier to cut out the rounds. Use a 5cm (2-inch) round cutter to stamp out up to 25 individual cakes.

2   Brush the top and sides of the cakes with boiled apricot jam. Knead and roll a ball of marzipan on a lightly dusted work surface to a thickness of 3mm (⅛ inch). Cut into squares large enough to cover the top and sides of each cake and gently lay over the cakes and press into shape.

3   Use a 6cm (2½-inch) cutter placed over the cake and marzipan to trim and neaten. Brush the marzipan with brandy or cooled boiled water.

4   Knead and roll a ball of white fondant sugar paste on a lightly dusted work surface to a thickness of 3mm (⅛ inch). Cut into squares as before and lay over the cakes. Shape and trim with a 7cm (2¾-inch) round cutter. Smooth the top and sides of the cakes with 2 icing smoothers and leave to firm.

## TO DECORATE THE CAKES

1   Cut a length of ribbon to fit around the base of each cake and fix in position with royal icing.

2   Fit 2 small piping bags with No. 2 nozzles and either white or coloured royal icing, mixed to the consistency of freshly whipped double cream. Holding the piping bag at a 90-degree angle to the cake and slightly away from the surface, pipe random pearls over the top and sides of each cake. Leave to set.

### TOP TIP

Choose your favourite
cake flavour as the base –
as long as it is chilled when you
cover the individuals to make
them easier to handle.

LAYER CAKES

## TO MAKE THE HEART PICKS

1   Roll a ball of fondant sugar paste to a thickness of 5–7mm (¼–½ inch) – use different colours to complement the crown cakes. Lay a sheet of cling film over the surface and press a heart cutter down into the paste. The cling film will gently stretch creating a rounded smooth edge to the heart.

2   Carefully remove the cling film and insert a cocktail stick in the base. Leave to firm until set.

3   Use the same royal icing to decorate each heart with delicate pearls and leave to set. To finish, tie a ribbon and bow around each heart and trim the ends.

These heart picks can be made up to 2 months in advance and stored in a sealed cake box away from bright lights to avoid them fading.

# SINGLE-TIER PEARL CAKE

*I love the simplicity of this design on a single tier cake. The pearls and stars showcase the exquisite craftsmanship of hand piping. This technique will challenge your hand piping but once mastered can be recreated using many different shapes and colours to maximum effect.*

**Makes 1 x 20cm (8 inch) cake**

*For the cake*

1 x 20cm (8 inch) cake of your choice,
  covered with a crumb coat of
  buttercream

Icing sugar, for dusting

750g (1lb 11oz) fondant sugar paste

1 quantity of Royal Icing (see page 199)

grosgrain ribbon to fit around the base
  of the cake

**TO DECORATE THE CAKE**

1   Bake your favourite cake of any shape.

2   Knead the fondant sugar paste and roll out on a clean work surface lightly dusted with icing sugar to a thickness of 4-5mm. Carefully lift and use to cover the cake. Shape into position and smooth with a cake icing smoother. Trim the excess.

3   Make a heart template to fit the top of the cake. Use a scribe around the shape on the top of the cake. Fill piping bags with different coloured royal icing and also fit one bag with a star nozzle No. 5. Pipe pearls and stars outside the heart template and spreading down the sides of the cake.

4   Fix a length of grosgrain ribbon around the base of the cake. Leave to firm until set.

## TOP TIPS

You can choose to pipe everything inside the template – or outside. For a more dramatic finish, consider piping both inside and out choosing contrasting colours. Change the template to suit the occasion – this could be a star, block initials, flags, a flower or even a teddy bear. Change the colour of icing and contrast with a cake board in a different colour – consider piping pearls around the cake board, too.

# MULTI-TIERED BUBBLES CAKE

*To take this effect onto a multi-tiered cake I have baked 10cm (4 inch), 15cm (6 inch), 20cm (8 inch) and 25cm (10 inch) cakes – but choose your favourite sizes, shapes and flavours to suit your celebration. The effect is a vibrant, fresh, textured cake. Hand-piping so many pearls is time consuming but it is worth it for the stunning showstopper finish.*

**Makes 1 x multi-tier cake**

*For the cake*

4 different-size layer cakes – I have used 10cm (4 inch), 15cm (6 inch), 20cm (8 inch) and 25cm (10 inch)

marzipan or buttercream of your choice, to cover all 4 cakes

*For the decoration*

3.5kg (7lb 14oz) yellow fondant sugar paste

ribbon to fit around the bottom and top tiers

1 quantity of Royal Icing (see page 199), reserving some for the heart decoration

food colouring gels of your choice

*For the heart decoration*

100g (3½oz) yellow fondant sugar paste mixed

100g (3½oz) gum paste

## TO DECORATE THE CAKE

1 Prepare the tiers by placing each cake on boards of matching sizes and either covering with marzipan or buttercream and then chilling until firm.

2 Knead and roll the yellow fondant sugar paste and cover the tiers one at a time, trimming and smoothing each cake. Leave to firm overnight.

3 Once the tiers have set and firmed, insert 6 dowelling rods evenly spaced into each tier, with the exception of the top tier. Mark the top of the cake on each rod. Remove one tier's set of rods at a time and trim the set so they are all the same length – if your cake is a little uneven you may find some rods are cut slightly shorter or longer than the mark to ensure they are all the same length. This will level your cake as they are stacked. Best to err on the side of shorter than longer – the cake can sink a little way into the tier below but better that way than wobbling on stilts above the top of the cake. Repeat with all tiers and fix the tiers in position with a smear of royal icing.

4 Fix a length of ribbon around the base of the top and bottom tiers with royal icing.

5 Using royal icing, decorate the cakes and base board with multi-coloured pearls using a series of No. 2 and 3 nozzles.

## TO MAKE THE HEART DECORATION

1 Mix the yellow fondant sugar paste with the gum paste to strengthen and roll out to a thickness of 1cm (½ inch).

2 Make a heart template and a sharp blade or large heart cutter to cut out the heart and insert a dowelling rod in the base.

3 Leave to firm at least overnight (but it can be made up to 2 weeks in advance) and then hand-pipe pearls over the surface. For a more professional finish, leave to set and then turn over and hand pipe the back of the heart as well.

4 Insert in the top tier to finish. Ta-da!

# CELEBRATION CAKES

# RUFFLE-TRUFFLE PIÑATA CAKE

*The classic piñata features a hard candy, chocolate or paper shell that is ceremonially bashed with gusto to reveal a waterfall of sweet treats. Use your imagination to fill and decorate your piñata cake once you've mastered the basics. Invest in a hemisphere tin and let your creativity flourish! This adult ruffle-truffle features a chocolate cake, filled with chocolates and decorated with chocolate buttercream ruffles.*

**Serves 12**

*For the sponge*

275g (10oz) unsalted butter, softened

275g (10oz) golden caster sugar

5 large eggs, beaten (weigh the eggs to ensure you have the same weight as the butter and sugar: 275g/10oz)

1 tbsp vanilla bean paste

235g (8½oz) self-raising flour

1½ tsp baking powder

40g (1½oz) cocoa powder

70–100ml (3–3½fl oz) milk

80g (3oz) dark chocolate chips

*For the chocolate buttercream*

250g (9oz) butter, softened

500g (1lb 2oz) golden icing sugar

250g (9oz) Chocolate Ganache (see page 15)

*For the decoration*

2 family packs of chocolate Minstrels

### TOP TIP

Blend enough chocolate ganache with the buttercream to achieve a rich, intense, smooth chocolate buttercream that can easily be hand-piped.

## TO MAKE THE SPONGE

1   Preheat the oven to 160°C fan (180°C/350°F/Gas 4). Spray a 20cm (8-inch) hemisphere tin with quick-release spray – or brush with melted butter and dust with flour.

2   Cream the butter and sugar together until pale and fluffy. Add the beaten eggs a little at a time until fully incorporated. Add the vanilla bean paste.

3   Sift in the flour, baking powder and cocoa powder. Add the milk to create a dropping consistency. Stir in the chocolate chips.

4   Spoon into the prepared tin and level the surface. Place the tin (stood inside the 15cm/6-inch ring) in the oven and bake for 1 hour 10 minutes until risen, golden brown and set – a skewer inserted in the centre should come out clean.

5   Remove from the oven and leave the tin to stand in the ring on a wire rack for 10 minutes. Turn the cake out upside down onto a wire rack to cool completely. The cake should instantly drop out of the tin. Wrap loosely in cling film and chill before filling.

## TO MAKE THE CHOCOLATE BUTTERCREAM

1   Cream the butter and icing sugar together in a large bowl until pale and light. Add the ganache and beat to make a smooth chocolate buttercream. Any excess ganache can be kept in the fridge for 2 weeks or up to 3 months in the freezer.

CELEBRATION CAKES

**TO ASSEMBLE THE CAKE**

1  Slice the cake horizontally into three sections. Remove the domed lid and set aside.

2  Place a small bowl over the two stacked base layers together and cut around it with a small, sharp knife. Remove the centres and save for making cake pops, trifle or enjoy with a cup of tea while you make the rest of the cake! Separate the layers so you end up with two rings and one domed top.

3  Place the base ring either on a cake plate or stand or on a larger cake board lined with sugar paste. (I used a 35cm/14-inch round cake board and lined this at least one day before decorating the cake so it had time to completely firm up and dry).

4  Spread the top of the ring with buttercream. Add the second ring and fill the hole in the centre with the chocolate Minstrels.

5  Spread the top of the ring with buttercream and then place the domed lid into position. Cover the whole of the top of the cake with buttercream using a small crank handled palette knife and optional flexible smoother. Chill until firm to the touch before covering and decorating.

**TO DECORATE THE CAKE**

1  Fit a large piping bag with a teardrop nozzle and fill with the remaining buttercream. Place the covered cake on a turntable.

2  Starting at the base, with the nozzle held horizontally against the cake, and with the thicker part of the teardrop against the cake and the thinner end away, swizzle the piping bag in an up/down motion as you apply pressure at the back of the bag and move the cake around on the turntable. This doesn't have to be perfect, or precise. Simply swizzle up and down as you work around and up the cake to the very top in the centre. Turn the cake on the cake stand rather than turning the piping bag. Refrigerate the cake until firm.

The cake will keep for up to 5 days in the refrigerator. Remove from the fridge up to 1 hour before serving – best served at room temperature. The cake has to be built and decorated on a cake board – don't be tempted to transfer it onto a board or plate once it is decorated because the base is hollow!

# PIRATE PIÑATA CAKE

*Ahoy there shipmates and shiver me timbers! Calling all you sea-faring folk ready to walk the plank for a slice or two of this fun pirate pinata cake – complete with a hidden secret stash of chocolate coin treasure. X definitely marks the spot!*

**Serves 12**

1 x Ruffle-Truffle Piñata Cake sponge (see page 150)

*For the chocolate buttercream*
175g (6oz) unsalted butter, softened
350g (12oz) icing sugar
75g (3oz) Chocolate Ganache (see page 15)

*For the decoration*
1.2kg (2¾lb) sugar paste (400g/14oz black for the cake board, eye patch and moustache, 200g/7oz red for the bandana, 30g/1¼oz white for the eyes and white polka dots, remainder for skin)
icing sugar, for dusting
1 metre (3.2ft) of 15mm (½-inch) wide black ribbon
300g (11oz) gold foiled chocolate coins
10g (½oz) gum paste (for the earring)
gold lustre spray

icing sugar, for dusting

## TO MAKE THE CAKE AND BUTTERCREAM
1   Make the sponge following the instructions on page 150.
2   Make the buttercream following the instructions on page 150.

## TO COVER THE CAKE BOARD
1   Knead the black sugar paste on a clean work surface until soft and pliable. Lightly dust the work surface with icing sugar and then roll the paste out to a diameter of just larger than 35cm (14 inches). Brush the cake board with cool water using a pastry brush. Lift the icing into position and smooth with a cake smoother. Trim the edges with a small, sharp knife. Leave to set and firm, ideally overnight. To get ahead you can over the board up to a week in advance.
2   Fix a length of black ribbon around the edge of the cake board and fix in position with a glue stick.

## TO DECORATE THE CAKE
1   When you are ready to cover the cake, build, fill and buttercream the cake into position on the base board using the gold foiled coins following the instructions on page 153.
2   Carefully cover the cake with a thin crumb coat of buttercream using a small palette knife. Refrigerate for 10 minutes.
3   Knead the skin-coloured sugar paste on a clean work surface until soft and pliable. Lightly dust the work surface with icing sugar and then roll the paste out to a diameter just larger than the cake (about 30cm/12 inches). Lift the icing into position and smooth with a cake smoother. Trim the edges with a small, sharp knife.
4   Fashion two ears and fix onto the side of the head, against the base board. Make the nose and fix into position with a little water. Use a small knife to create the mouth.

→

CELEBRATION CAKES

5   Indent the position of the eyes with a ball tool and create one eye and pupil and one eye patch. Make the moustache and beard. Roll a thin piece of black sugar paste to create the string of the eye patch and fix this in position from one ear. These can all be fixed in position with a little cooled water using a paint brush.

6   Knead and roll out a piece of red sugar paste. Stud with little white balls of sugar paste and then place a sheet of greaseproof paper over the top of the icing. Use a rolling pin to roll and press the white circles into the red paste to make the bandana.

7   Brush the top of the head with cooled, boiled water using a pastry brush. Trim one edge of the red paste to create the sharp edge of the bandana and lift into position. Shape and trim with a sharp knife. Use a small piece of the red paste to create the bandana knot and fix into position over one ear.

8   Make an earring using gum paste. I stood mine over a large nozzle to firm. Spray with gold lustre and then fix into position (you will need to trim a little out of the earring using a sharp knife) using a little water.

This cake will keep for up to 3 days at room temperature and should not be refrigerated. Not suitable for freezing.

# UNICORN PIÑATA CAKE

*This cake is every bit as mythical and magical as its namesake. The vanilla sponge is studded with coloured sugar strands before baking and the cavity is filled with jelly sweets. This design will showcase your sugar craft skills and is a clever adaptation of one of the biggest recent trends in cake designs.*

**Serves 12**

*For the sponge*

275g (10oz) unsalted butter, softened

275g (10oz) golden caster sugar

5 large eggs, beaten (weigh the eggs to ensure you have the same weight as the butter, sugar and flour: 275g/10oz)

1 tbsp vanilla bean paste

275g (10oz) self-raising flour

1 tsp baking powder

70-100ml (3-3½fl oz) milk (to create dropping consistency)

40g (1½oz) sprinkles

*For the buttercream*

200g (7oz) butter, softened

400g (14oz) icing sugar

2 tsp vanilla bean paste

*For the decoration*

900g (1lb) sugar paste (400g/14oz blue for the base board and 500g/1lb 2oz white for the cake)

250g (9oz) gum paste

gold or pearl lustre spray

hologram glitter

3 x 150g (5oz) family packs of jelly sweets

1 quantity of coloured Royal Icing (see page 199),

1 metre (3.2ft) of 15mm (½ inch) wide blue ribbon

icing sugar, for dusting

## TO MAKE THE CAKE AND BUTTERCREAM

1   Make the sponge following the instructions on page 150 omitting the cocoa and adding the sprinkles to the batter before spooning into the tin.

2   Make the buttercream by beating all of the ingredients together in a large bowl until smooth.

## TO DECORATE THE CAKE

1   Line the cake board using the blue sugar paste and fix on the ribbon following the instructions on page 155.

2   To make the horn, prepare 2 sausages of gum paste about 10cm (4 inches) in length and 2cm (¾ inch) wide. Twist and roll these together, taking one end thin to a point. Trim to size and insert a bamboo skewer in the base, leaving a length of 5cm (2 inches) to insert in the cake once set. Leave the horn to set and firm (I stood mine upright in a piece of sugar paste) and spray with gold or pearl lustre spray and dust with hologram glitter.

3   Prepare the ears in a similar way. Fashion two shapes from gum paste and insert cocktail sticks for support.

4   Use black sugar paste to fashion the eyes. Roll thin strips or tubes and cut into eyelashes. Fix in position using a small, damp paintbrush and leave to dry.

5   When you are ready to cover the cake, build and buttercream the cake in position on the base board and fill with sweet treats. Cover the cake with a layer of buttercream using a small cranked handle palette knife and chill until firm.

6   Knead the sugar paste on a clean work surface until soft and pliable. Lightly dust the work surface with icing sugar and then roll the paste out to a diameter just larger than the cake (about 30cm/12 inches). Lift the icing into position and smooth with a cake smoother. Trim the edges with a small, sharp knife.

→

CELEBRATION CAKES

**TOP TIP**

Pipe extra swirls and shapes onto waxed paper and allowed these to firm overnight. Prise them from the paper using a small, sharp knife and add these to the mane to build 3D depth to the cake.

7   Fit a piping bag with a 2D nozzle and will with two colours of royal icing. Fit another with a 195C nozzle and fill with coloured icing.

8   Insert the horn and ears into the cake. Fix the eyes in position either with a little royal icing or brush the base of the eyes with a little water using a fine paintbrush.

9   Pipe swirls of royal icing onto the cake starting in front of the horn, then moving around the ears and then over the top and down the side of the cake to create the mane. Finish on the cake board.

This cake will keep for up to 3 days at room temperature and should not be refrigerated. Not suitable for freezing.

# CHOCOLATE FUDGE HEART CAKE

*A heart shaped cake is not just for Valentine's Day! There are so many occasions when a cake in the shape of heart says how much you love someone. To give you many options I have created one recipe of a moist chocolate fudge cake than can either be just topped, or smothered in chocolate frosting and decorated with a range of treats - from fresh fruits to biscuits, sweets (the ultimate "Sweetheart") or hand moulded sugar roses. J'adore!*

**Makes 1 x 20cm (8 inch) cake**

*For the sponge*
200g (7oz) plain flour
150g (5oz) golden caster sugar
150g (5oz) soft brown sugar
50g (2oz) cocoa powder
1½ tsp baking powder
½ tsp salt
80ml (3fl oz) sunflower oil
1 large egg
1 tbsp vanilla extract
190ml (6½fl oz) whole milk
190ml (6½fl oz) coffee
    (2 shots espresso topped up with
    boiling water or 2 tsp instant coffee
    powder)

*For the chocolate frosting*
75g (3oz) cocoa powder
100g (3½oz) golden icing sugar
60g (2½oz) unsalted butter, softened
1 tsp vanilla extract
50ml (2fl oz) milk

*For the decoration (choose one
or more of the options below)*
600g fresh strawberries
3 x 154g (5oz) packets of Oreo cookies,
    each biscuit carefully cut in half
    with a serrated knife
300g favourite sweets (including
    jelly sweets, Smarties, chocolate
    honeycomb balls)

## TO MAKE THE SPONGE

1   Preheat the oven to 170°C fan (190°C/375°F/Gas 5). Lightly grease a 20cm (8 inch) heart-shaped cake tin and the line sides and base with non-stick baking paper.

2   Sift the flour, sugars, cocoa powder, baking powder and salt in a large bowl.

3   In a separate bowl, whisk together the oil, egg, vanilla extract, milk and coffee and then whisk into the dry ingredients until fully mixed and glossy.

4   Pour the batter into the prepared cake tin and bake for 40 minutes for a fudge texture and until a skewer inserted in the centre comes out clean.

5   Remove from the oven and leave to cool in the tin for 20 minutes. Transfer the cake to a wire rack and leave to cool, then chill for 30 minutes before frosting.

## TO MAKE THE CHOCOLATE FROSTING

1   Put all the ingredients in a large bowl and beat with a wooden spoon until you have a smooth, thick frosting.

## TO ASSEMBLE THE CAKE

1   Cover the top and then the sides of the cake with frosting and smooth with a palette knife or cake scraper. This will create a small collar to support the fruit.

2   Arrange the strawberries on top of the cake to fill the heart shape. Alternatively, simply spread the frosting on the top only, then push the halved cookies into the frosting around the edge of the heart shape, or scatter with the sweet mixture depending on which topping you have chosen.

This cake will keep for 3–5 days at room temperature without the strawberries. The base is suitable for freezing – defrost at room temperature and then decorate.

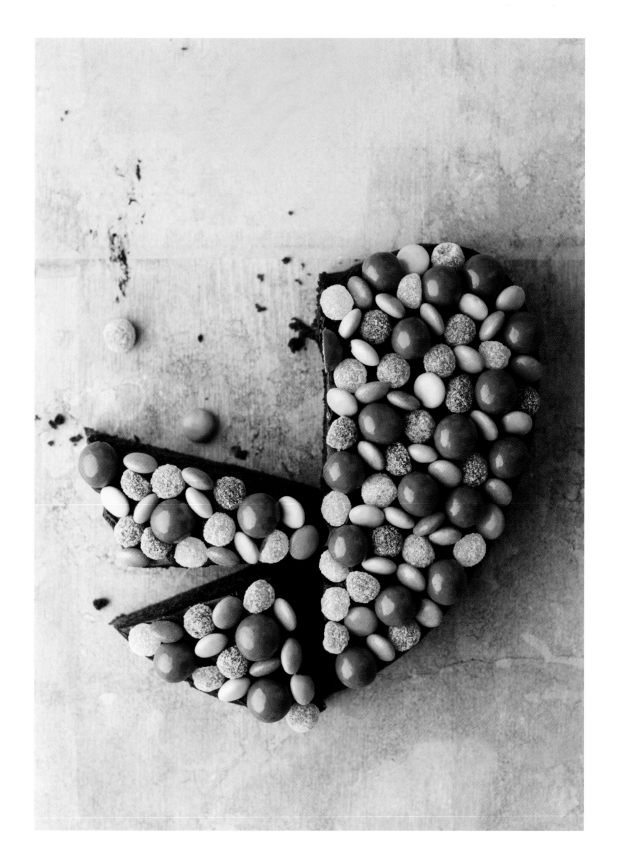

# CHOCOLATE FUDGE HEART CAKE WITH SUGAR ROSES

*A dozen red roses say "I love you" - so how much would you love someone to cover this cake with a hundred hand moulded red rose buds? Made from red fondant sugar paste, they can be made well in advance to dress this moist, fresh baked chocolate cake. Elevate the everyday to the stratospheric showstopper!*

**Makes 1 x 20cm (8 inch) cake**

1 x Chocolate Fudge Heart Cake
    sponge (see page 162)

*For the chocolate frosting*
150g (5oz) cocoa powder
200g (7oz) golden icing sugar
120g (4oz) unsalted butter, softened
2 tsp vanilla extract
100ml (3½ fl oz) milk

*For the decoration*
Hand-moulded red sugar roses (see
    page 136) – I made 100 rose buds to
    cover this cake
3 petal rose buds

## TO MAKE THE CHOCOLATE FROSTING

Use the ingredients to make a smooth frosting following the instructions on page 162.

## TO ASSEMBLE THE CAKE

1   Chill the cake until firm.
2   Place the cake on a plate and cover the top and sides with frosting. Smooth with a palette knife or cake scraper.
3   Position the hand-moulded red sugar rosebuds, packed closely together to cover the surface of the cake.

This cake will keep for 3–5 days at room temperature without the strawberries. The base is suitable for freezing – defrost at room temperature and then decorate.

### TOP TIP

To make the rose buds, use 3 petals to achieve a uniform shape and size. You can make these up to 1 month in advance.

# PASSION FRUIT FLOWER CUPCAKES

*I first saw these Nifty Nozzles at Cake International, a cake decorators' emporium and competition showcase. They are extremely effective for decorating cakes – although it takes a little practice to master the technique. The delicate mango cupcakes are complemented by a super zingy passion fruit curd and decorated with silky-sweet vanilla flavoured, coloured buttercream.*

**Makes 12 cupcakes**

*For the cupcakes*

200g (7oz) unsalted butter

200g (7oz) golden caster sugar

4 large eggs, beaten (weigh the eggs to
   ensure you have the same weight as
   the butter, sugar and flour: 200g/7oz)

2 tsp vanilla extract

200g (7oz) self-raising flour

30g (1¼oz) freeze-dried mango powder

40ml (1½fl oz) milk

*For the passion fruit curd*

8 passion fruit (135g/4½oz passion
   fruit seeds)

225g (8oz) golden caster sugar

3 medium eggs and 1 egg yolk

90g (3¼oz) unsalted butter, chilled,
   cut into 1cm (½ inch) cubes

juice of 1 lemon

*For the vanilla buttercream*

250g (9oz) unsalted butter, softened

500g (1lb 2oz) icing sugar

2 tbsp vanilla extract

1–2 tbsp sweetened condensed milk

*For the decoration*

selection of food colouring gels –
   orange and yellow, lilac and ivory, greens

selection of nifty nozzles for blooms
   and various leaf nozzles

## TO MAKE THE CUPCAKES

1   Preheat the oven to 170°C fan (190°C/375°F/Gas 5). Place 12 cupcake cases in a shallow baking tray.

2   Cream the butter and sugar together in a large bowl until pale and fluffy. Add the beaten eggs a little at a time until fully incorporated and then stir in the vanilla extract.

3   Sift the flour and mango powder together and fold into the batter with the milk until smooth with a dropping consistency.

4   Divide the batter equally between the cupcake cases.

5   Bake the cupcakes for 20 minutes until baked, risen and golden.

6   Remove from the oven and leave to cool on a wire rack.

## TO MAKE THE PASSION FRUIT CURD

1   Cut the passion fruit in half and scoop out all the flesh and seeds. Place in a large saucepan together with the sugar, eggs, butter and lemon.

2   Heat over a medium–low heat, stirring all the time. Do not let the curd boil. As it gradually thickens it will begin to coat the back of a wooden spoon. Remove from the heat and transfer to a clean bowl or jar.

3   Store in a clean jar in the refrigerator until needed and consume within 2 weeks.

## TO MAKE THE VANILLA BUTTERCREAM

1   Cream the butter and sugar together with the vanilla extract in a large bowl. Add sufficient condensed milk for a semi-soft piping consistency. Divide into bowls and colour each portion as desired.

$\longrightarrow$

## TO ASSEMBLE THE CUPCAKES

1   Use a cupcake corer to remove a plug of cake and spoon 2 very generous teaspoons of passion fruit curd inside each one. Replace the plug of cake.

2   Smear a fine layer of vanilla buttercream over the surface of each cupcake to seal.

3   Fit a large piping bag with a Nifty Nozzle and fill with one colour buttercream. Fill a separate piping bag (with no nozzle) with a contrasting/complementing colour. Snip off the end of this piping bag and then insert the piping bag right into the centre and all the way to the nozzle of the first filled bag. Firmly squeeze this buttercream as you withdraw the piping bag (which can then be discarded or reused) – leaving the second colour through the centre of the first. Twist the end of the piping bag so you are ready to pipe.

4   Place the nozzle at a 90 degree angle to the cake and apply firm pressure as you gently tease the bag upwards creating the flower. Release the pressure as you finish and snatch the tip away – leaving a perfect bloom.

5   Decorate the cupcakes with hand-piped flowers using a variety of colours and nozzles and then fill any gaps with a green leaf nozzle. This should be held with the point facing the direction of the leaf and pressure applied with a very gentle side-to-side wiggle before releasing the pressure to create the perfect leaf

6   Refrigerate the cupcakes to firm but serve at room temperature.

These cupcakes will keep for up to 3 days and are suitable for freezing. Place in a suitable container and chill to firm before placing in the freezer. To defrost, remove from the freezer and bring up to room temperature.

# MOTHERING SUNDAY MANGO AND PASSION FRUIT CAKE

*Once you have mastered this piping technique you can stun your family and friends with this hand-piped showstopper layer cake – perfect for Mothering Sunday. The soft mango-flavoured cakes are layered with heavenly vanilla buttercream and passion fruit curd.*

**Serves 12**

1 quantity of Passion Fruit Curd
    (see page 168)
2 quantities of Vanilla Buttercream
    (see page 168)

*For the sponges*
275g (10oz) unsalted butter
275g (10oz) golden caster sugar
5 large eggs, beaten (weigh the eggs
    to ensure you have the same
    weight as the butter, sugar and
    flour: 275g/10oz)
3 tsp vanilla extract
275g (10oz) self-raising flour
40g (1½oz) freeze-dried mango
    powder
70ml (3fl oz) milk

*For the decoration*
selection of food colouring gels –
    orange and yellow, lilac and ivory,
    greens
selection of Nifty Nozzles for blooms
    and various leaf nozzles

## TO MAKE THE SPONGES

1   Preheat oven to 170°C fan (190°C/375°F/Gas 5). Grease and line the base and sides of three 20cm (8-inch) round, shallow cake tins and grease a 600ml (1 pint) pudding basin.
2   Using the sponge ingredients, prepare the batter following the instructions on page 168. Divide the batter equally between the three tins and pudding basin. I found the 20cm (8 inch) tins each held 320g (11½oz) batter and the basin 200g (7oz).
3   Bake the cakes for 20 minutes and the pudding basin for 25 minutes until risen and golden. Remove from the oven and leave to cool on a wire rack. Turn out after 10 minutes and leave to cool before wrapping in cling film and chilling before filling.

## TO ASSEMBLE THE CAKE

1   Place the base layer on a cake board, plate or stand and spread the surface with vanilla buttercream using a palette knife. Create a well in the centre and fill with passion fruit curd. Spread this out to level and place the second layer on top. Repeat with the buttercream and passion fruit curd then apply the third layer.
2   Spread a generous layer of buttercream over the top and sides and smooth with a palette knife and side smoother.
3   Place the domed cake on the top in the centre and cover with buttercream. This will be completely covered with the flowers so it doesn't have to be perfectly smooth.
4   Decorate the dome with the hand-piped flowers following the instructions on page 168, starting at the base. Try to pipe the flowers in clusters interspersed with other colours and then finish with the green leaves to fill any gaps and balance the shape.
5   Refrigerate the cake to firm but serve at room temperature.

The cake will keep for up to 3 days and is suitable for freezing. Place in a suitable container and chill to firm before placing in the freezer.
To defrost, remove from the freezer and bring up to room temperature.

# MARBLED EASTER BISCUITS

*The bank holiday Easter weekend is the perfect time to begin the social calendar –*
*a time to invite family and friends for coffee as the first flowers bloom and the weather*
*is finally a little warmer and certainly brighter. The traditional Easter biscuit is a*
*lightly spiced butter biscuit with currants, dredged with sugar and eaten plain with*
*tea or coffee. I like to make these simple iced biscuits for added colour and flavour.*

**Makes 30–40 biscuits**

*For the biscuits*
200g (7oz) unsalted butter, softened
200g (7oz) golden caster sugar
1 medium egg, beaten
1 tsp vanilla powder
   or 2 tsp vanilla bean paste
400g (14oz) plain flour, plus extra
   for dusting
1 heaped tsp baking powder

*For the glace icing*
300g (11oz) icing sugar
2–4 tbsp lemon, lime or orange juice
yellow, green and orange food
   colouring gels

## TO MAKE THE BISCUITS

1  Cream the butter and sugar together in a stand mixer until light and fluffy.
2  Add the beaten egg and vanilla until fully incorporated and then add the flour and baking powder. Mix just until the dough comes together. Wrap in cling film and chill for 30 minutes.
3  Preheat the oven to 180°C fan (200°C/400°F/Gas 4). Line a baking tray with non-stick baking paper.
4  Knead the dough on a lightly floured work surface and then roll out gently to a thickness of 3–4mm (⅛ inch). Stamp out shapes using Easter-shaped cutters. Place on the prepared baking tray, leaving a little space between the biscuits.
5  Bake for 8–10 minutes until lightly golden brown on the edges. Remove from the oven, leave to cool for a few minutes and then lift on to a wire rack with a palette knife to cool completely.

## TO MAKE THE GLACE ICING

1  Mix the icing sugar with the lemon, lime or orange juice to a free flowing consistency but not too stiff or too runny. Divide into 4 bowls and colour 3 of the bowls yellow, green and orange, leaving one white.

## TO DECORATE THE BISCUITS

1  Spoon the coloured icing into 4 piping bags. Place the biscuits on a wire rack over a sheet of non-stick baking paper.
2  Working one colour at a time, snip off the end off the piping bags and gently swizzle icing over the biscuits. Take the next colour and fill in more of the biscuit. Repeat until all the colours are used and the biscuits are covered.
3  Use a cocktail stick to gently marble the icing and clean around the edge of each biscuit. Leave to set.

The biscuits will keep for up to 14 days once decorated if they are stored in a cake box or lightly sealed container.

# HAND-DECORATED EASTER BISCUITS

*These fully hand-decorated Easter biscuits are a fabulous way to showcase your skill and creativity. Cute, fresh, fun and frivolous, they bring joy and a sunny smile to your Easter table. They can be presented individually as gifts or even made into an Easter wreath.*

**Makes 30–40 biscuits**

1 quantity of Easter Biscuits
(see page 175)

*For the decorations*
coloured fondant sugar paste
(allow 30g/1¼oz per biscuit)
1 quantity of Royal Icing (see page 199)
in different colours
sugar flowers (optional)
colour dusts mixed with a little
rejuvenator spirit or cooled, boiled
water, for painting (optional)
yellow coloured gum paste

## TO DECORATE THE BISCUITS

1  Once the biscuits are cool, roll out different colours of sugar paste fondant. Cut out shapes using the same cutters as you used for the biscuits (see page 175).
2  Dot royal icing on the biscuits and fix the sugar paste cut-outs in position.
3  Add extra coloured hand-piped pearls around the edge of the biscuits using a No. 2 nozzle and your chosen coloured royal icing.
4  For the daisies – pipe a series of white pearls joined together with a yellow centre.
5  For the chicks – pipe the eyes and feet with black royal icing and add a hand-piped orange beak.
6  For the swirls – starting at the centre of the biscuit, with one colour, hand pipe a thick swirl to the outer edge. Fill between with a second swirl in a contrasting colour.
7  For the daffodils – hand mould the daffodils from yellow coloured gum paste using a daffodil cutter. Leave to dry overnight. Blend the colour dusts with the rejuvenator spirit or water and brush long leaves and stems onto the biscuit. Fix the daffodils in position with royal icing.
8  For the buttercups – make tiny yellow 3-petal bud flowers from sugarpaste and leave to firm. Pipe 3 green leaves using a leaf-nozzle and position the flowers in the centre.

The biscuits will keep for up to 14 days once decorated if they are stored in a cake box or lightly sealed container.

# CHOCOLATE MARBLED EASTER EGGS

*There is nothing more charming and thoughtful than taking the time to make homemade Easter eggs. It's a tradition I introduced with my boys who each made one for the other, loading them with their favourite sweet treats. This 'Rocky Road' version is stuffed with marshmallows, honeycomb and chocolate covered mini eggs. Now, where is that Easter Bunny?*

**Makes 2 eggs**

sunflower oil, for brushing

275g (10oz) unsalted butter

150g (5oz) golden syrup

225g (8oz) dark chocolate
  (70% cocoa solids)

130g (4¼oz) Maltesers

100g (3½oz) mini chocolate eggs

40g (1½oz) mini marshmallows

100g (3½oz) broken rich tea biscuits

100g (3½oz) broken digestive biscuits

25g (1oz) melted white chocolate

**TOP TIP**

Personalise your egg with your favourite biscuits, sweets or chocolates.

## TO MAKE THE EASTER EGG

1  Start by brushing 2 large plastic Easter egg moulds (165 x 110mm/ 6½ x 4¼ inch) with a little sunflower oil and place them in the refrigerator to chill.

2  Place the butter, syrup and chocolate in a large saucepan and melt together gently over a medium–low heat. Leave to cool.

3  Measure the remaining dry ingredients together in a large bowl. Pour over the melted chocolate liquid (reserving 3–4 tablespoons) and stir until fully coated.

4  Fill a piping bag with the melted white chocolate and swizzle over the base and sides of the mould. Return to the refrigerator until the chocolate has set.

5  Brush the moulds with a little of the reserved melted chocolate syrup. Spoon the chocolate biscuit mixture into each egg until packed full but not overloaded.

6  Spoon the remaining chocolate liquid over the back of the eggs to help level and fill any spaces.

7  Cover and wrap each egg mould with cling film pressing down flat. Refrigerate until firm – this can take 2 hours, but they can be kept in the fridge until required for up to 14 days.

## TO FINISH

1  Simply remove the egg from the refrigerator and allow to stand at room temperature for 5 minutes. Remove the cling film and carefully but firmly press the mould to release the suction and the egg will easily drop out.

Best served chilled. The eggs will keep for up to 14 days.

CELEBRATION CAKES

# VENETIAN EASTER EGGS

*I love, love, love this design and have recreated it in a million different colourways. It is impressive and stylish and makes a gorgeous gift. The rose, leaves and rolled pearls can all be made in advance and stored. As an extra, extra special treat, position this egg straight on top of a decorated cake.*

**Makes 2 eggs**

2 x Chocolate Marbled Easter Eggs
(see page 179), chilled

*For the decoration*
100g (3½oz) brown fondant sugar
    paste, for the board
1 metre of 15mm (½ inch) wide ribbon
350g–500g (12oz–1lb 2oz) fondant
    sugar paste (including rolled pearls)
    in two colours
icing sugar, for dusting
4 tbsp Royal Icing (see page 199)
gold lustre spray
30g (1¼oz) pink fondant sugar paste,
    for the rose

## TOP TIP

There should be enough tackiness in the sugar paste for the pearls to adhere and set as the paste firms – but if they feel a little unstable fix each in position with a dot of royal icing.

## TO ASSEMBLE THE EGG

1   Start by lining the cake board. Knead and roll the 100g (3½oz) of fondant sugar paste into a 23cm (9 inch) circle; brush the board with cooled, boiled water and then smooth the icing in place. Trim the edges with a sharp knife and then fix ribbon around the edge using a glue stick to hold it in place. When you are ready to cover the egg, remove the mould from the fridge, wait 5 minutes then release the egg. Place on a sheet of baking paper.

2   Knead one colour of the sugar paste until pliable and roll to a thickness of 2–3mm (⅛ inch) on a lightly dusted work surface, large enough to cover the egg. Place over the egg (you will not need anything to make it stick) and press into shape. Smooth with your hands and trim around with a sharp knife. Neaten the edges using a smoother and then lift the whole egg with a sharp knife and place on the lined board.

3   Without using any additional icing sugar, pinch and roll large pearls of your chosen colour fondant sugar paste and fix immediately into positon around the edge of the egg. If you find they are not sticking, use a little royal icing to secure.

4   Fit a piping bag with a No. 2 nozzle and and fill the white royal icing. Mark the egg into 8 even sections at the base – I tend to mark front and back, side to side and then in between each of these. Hand pipe a double loop between each marked point and finish with a large pearl at the top of each. Leave until set.

5   Fix a sheet of waxed paper onto a workboard. Fit a piping bag with a No. 69 leaf nozzle and fill with white royal icing. Pipe a series of leaves on the work board and spray with gold lustre and leave to set overnight.

6   Release from the sheet with a small knife and fix into position on the top of the egg with a dot of royal icing.

7   Make the rose from fondant sugar paste following the instructions on page 136. Fix in position with royal icing.

Store and serve at room temperature. The eggs will keep for up to 14 days.

CELEBRATION CAKES

# TRICK OR TREAT MUMMY BISCUITS

*In recent years, Halloween has grown hugely in popularity – with schools and neighbourhoods celebrating the occasion with Halloween parties and the obligatory trick or treating. Fear not, for I have some delicious treats in store for you. For my everyday bake these Mummy Biscuits are very quick to make. The simple vanilla biscuit dough is stamped out using a gingerbread cutter and then decorated with white royal icing.*

**Makes 24 biscuits**

*For the biscuits*

200g (7oz) unsalted butter, at
    room temperature

200g (7oz) golden caster sugar

1 large egg, beaten

1 tsp vanilla bean paste

400g (14oz) plain flour, plus extra
    for rolling

1 tsp baking powder

*For the royal icing*

2 egg whites

300g (11oz) icing sugar

½ tsp peppermint essence

black food colouring gel

## TO MAKE THE BISCUITS

1   Cream the butter and sugar together in a large bowl until pale and fluffy. Add the beaten egg and then stir in the vanilla bean paste.

2   Sift the flour and baking powder together and fold into the creamed mixture to form a dough. Wrap in cling film and allow to rest in the fridge for 30 minutes.

3   Preheat the oven to 180°C fan (200°C/400°F/Gas 6) and line 2 baking sheets with non-stick baking parchment.

4   Roll the dough out on a lightly floured work surface to a depth of 4mm (⅛ inch). Stamp out gingerbread men shapes and place on the baking tray spaced apart.

5   Bake for 8-10 minutes until baked and golden brown on the edges.

6   Leave to cool for 2 minutes before lifting out onto a wire rack to cool.

## TO DECORATE THE BISCUITS

1   Make the royal icing by whisking together the egg whites and icing sugar in a large bowl until it is thick and mallowy but still flows. Add a few drops of peppermint essence to flavour and remove 1 tablespoon to colour black.

2   Fill a piping bag fitted with a No. 3 nozzle with white royal icing and start by piping the 2 eyes into position. Fit a second piping bag with a No 1.5 nozzle and fill with the black royal icing and pipe the pupils so the mummies are all looking in different directions.

3   Pipe the white icing across the biscuit to create the Mummies' bandages. Leave to set for 2-4 hours.

The idea is to create small individual bakes for all those vampires, ghouls, zombies and witches that will be running wild on 31st October!

The biscuits will keep for 14 days if stored in an airtight container.

**A HALLOWEEN JOKE**

Q: Why do mummies make excellent spies?
A: Because they are good at keeping things under wraps!

# HALLOWEEN MINI ROLLS

*For the more glamourous witches and Count Draculas among you, these mini rolls offer a sophisticated treat for Halloween. They are more labour-intensive, but well worth the effort if you are looking for a more challenging bake. For a hidden surprise I have added popping candy to the buttercream. Each mini roll is fully enrobed in smooth chocolate and decorated with swizzles of coloured white chocolate. Not only that – they are devilishly moreish and by nature, gluten-free.*

**Makes 12 mini rolls**

*For the sponge*

150g (5oz) golden caster sugar, plus
    extra for dusting

6 large eggs, separated

50g (2oz) cocoa powder

*For the chocolate ganache*

150g (5oz) unsalted butter

300g (11oz) dark chocolate
    (70% cocoa solids)

75ml (3fl oz) double cream

*For the chocolate-orange buttercream*

150g (5oz) unsalted butter, at
    room temperature

300g (11oz) golden icing sugar

6–8 tbsp Chocolate Ganache
    (see above)

4 tbsp popping candy

1 tsp peppermint oil

1½ tsp orange oil (or grated zest of
    1 small orange)

*For the decoration*

200g (7oz) dark chocolate
    (70% cocoa solids)

200g (7oz) milk chocolate

60g (2½oz) white chocolate

tangerine orange food colouring gel

peppermint green food colouring gel

## TO MAKE THE SPONGE

1   Preheat the oven to 170°C fan (190°C/375°F/Gas 5) and line two 30 x 20cm (12 x 8-inch) rectangular Swiss roll tins with non-stick baking paper.

2   Place the sugar and egg yolks together in a large heatproof glass bowl and set over a saucepan of simmering water. Whisk until the mixture triples in size, is pale, light and silky and leaves a ribbon trail.

3   Remove from the heat and sift the cocoa into the bowl. Fold in with a spatula

4   Whisk the egg whites until soft peaks form and then spoon one-third into the cocoa batter. Stir carefully and then add the next third and fold in gently. Add the remaining egg white and fold until the batter is fully mixed.

5   Divide between the 2 tins and level the surface with the back of a metal spoon. Bake for 16-18 minutes until the surface springs back when pressed.

6   Meanwhile, soak 2 clean tea towels in cold water, wring out and lay on a clean work surface. Lay a sheet of non-stick baking paper on the surface of each and dust with a little golden caster sugar. I use 4 little dishes to hold the corners down.

7   As soon as the Swiss roll comes out of the oven, upturn the sponge onto the baking paper and carefully remove the paper that the cake was cooked on, tearing it in strips to protect the Swiss roll.

8   Starting from one of the short ends, roll the Swiss roll up with the paper inside until it reaches the middle. Turn it round and roll from the other short end to meet in the middle. Repeat with the second Swiss roll.

9   Wrap the Swiss rolls in the cold, damp tea towels and leave both to cool and chill.

→

### TO MAKE THE GANACHE

1  Place the butter and chocolate in a heatproof bowl and
   place in the microwave on medium heat for 1 minute to soften.
2  Bring the cream to the boil in a small saucepan and then pour
   over the chocolate and butter. Stir until fully mixed, smooth
   and velvety.

### TO MAKE THE CHOCOLATE-ORANGE BUTTERCREAM

1  Cream together the unsalted butter and golden icing sugar until
   light and fluffy.
2  Add the cooled ganache and stir until fully mixed. You can add
   more or less to suit your own taste. Stir in the popping candy.
3  Divide the buttercream between 2 bowls. Add the peppermint oil
   to one bowl and adjust to taste. Stir the orange oil or fresh orange
   zest into the other bowl and again adjust to taste.

### TO ASSEMBLE THE MINI ROLLS

1  Unravel one of the sponges from both ends – it should be nicely
   curled. While the Swiss roll is still on the baking paper, use a small
   palette knife to spread one of the buttercreams over the surface and
   right to the edges of the sponge. Carefully roll up the Swiss roll
   from the short ends to meet in the centre.
2  Cut the Swiss roll between the 2 long logs to separate. Repeat this
   process with the second Swiss roll, filling it with the other
   flavoured buttercream. Set all 4 long logs on a clean work board
   and place in the freezer for 20 minutes to firm.
3  Remove the logs from the freezer and use a sharp knife to trim the
   ends to neaten and sharpen.
4  Use a ruler to divide the logs into equal mini rolls. Cut each
   log with a sharp knife and position the mini rolls on a wire rack,
   well-spaced apart. Place the wire rack on a sheet of baking paper
   to catch the chocolate so it can be reheated and reused.
5  Melt the dark and milk chocolate together in a heatproof bowl
   over a saucepan of water. This makes a palatable chocolate for the
   mini rolls.
6  Transfer the chocolate to a jug and pour over each mini roll.
   Use a palette knife to ensure the ends are also fully covered.

### TO DECORATE THE MINI ROLLS

1   Place the white chocolate in a heatproof bowl and melt in the microwave or over a pan of simmering water.
2   Divide between 2 bowls and colour with either tangerine orange or peppermint green food colouring gel. Leave to cool until gently runny.
3   Spoon the melted chocolate into piping bags. Snip off the very ends. Swizzle the coloured chocolate back and forth across each of the mini rolls. Leave until set.
4   Use a sharp knife to remove the mini rolls from the rack.

These are best eaten on the day, but will keep for 2-3 days in an airtight container, in a cool place away from direct sunlight – like all vampires!

# CHRISTMAS CHOCOLATE BISCUIT CAKE

*Not everyone is a fan of traditional rich fruit Christmas cake, so this recipe is a perfect treat to excite your creativity and please your palate. Chocolate biscuit cake is a universal hit — not least because it requires no baking so can be easily made by even the humblest baker. But what about a ramped-up Christmas version with orange chocolate, ginger biscuits, crystallised ginger, dried cherries and cranberries? It is the ultimate sweet treat and so unbelievably tempting and satisfying.*

**Makes 24 pieces**

120g (4oz) digestive biscuits

120g (4oz) rich tea biscuits

100g (3½oz) ginger nut biscuits

100g (3½oz) roasted, salted almonds, roughly chopped

170g (6oz) mixed dried berries (cranberries, cherries, blueberries)

70g (3oz) finely chopped crystallised ginger

300g (11oz) dark orange chocolate

200g (7oz) golden syrup

375g (13oz) unsalted butter

icing sugar, for dusting

1   Line the base and sides of a 30 x 20cm (12 x 8 inch) rectangular baking tray with non-stick baking paper.

2   In a large bowl, roughly crush the biscuits and mix in the nuts, fruit and ginger.

3   Place the chocolate, syrup and butter in a large saucepan and heat gently until fully melted.

4   Pour the chocolate syrup over the biscuits and stir until all the ingredients are evenly coated.

5   Pour the mixture into the tin. Lay a sheet of cling film over the top and press firmly to seal. Refrigerate until firm. Cut into bite-sized squares and serve from the fridge dusted with a little icing sugar.

Store in the fridge in a tin or sealed container for up to 14 day. Suitable for freezing. Defrost in the fridge.

**TOP TIP**

For an extra festive flourish, load the surface with extra crushed chocolate biscuit treats before chilling. This is the perfect bake to serve Christmas guests who pop in unannounced but you may not want to share!

# CHOCOLATE BISCUIT WREATH CAKE

*Shape your festive chocolate biscuit mix in a bundt tin to make this stunning wreath covered with chocolate fondant and decorated with hand-decorated biscuits and iced poinsettia flowers. Serve from the fridge as an alternative to Christmas cake. The components for this cake can be made well in advance helping you to organise and plan for a festive event. It makes a very impressive festive gift.*

**Makes 1 x 25cm (10 inch) cake**

*For the wreath*
1 quantity of Christmas Chocolate
    Biscuit Cake mixture (see page 193)
sunflower oil, for brushing

*For the holly biscuits*
½ quantity of Gingerbread Biscuit
    dough (see page 199)
1 quantity of Royal Icing (see page 199)
green food colouring gel

*For the poinsettia flowers*
1 quantity of Royal Icing
    (see page 199), coloured red
3 tbsp Royal Icing (see page 199),
    coloured yellow

*For the decoration*
1kg (2¼lb) chocolate fondant sugar
    paste
icing sugar, for dusting
small red sugar pearls

## TO MAKE THE WREATH

1   Grease a 25cm (10 inch) bundt tin and line with cling film, making sure there are no gaps and the cling film comes up and over the outside of the tin. Lightly brush with sunflower oil.
2   Make the biscuit cake mix following the instructions on page 193.
3   Spoon the biscuit mixture into the tin, pressing down firmly with the back of a spoon. Bring the cling film over the top of the cake, seal and press down firmly. Place in the fridge until the cake is completely firm – this can take 4 hours but it can also be made up to a week in advance.
4   Once the cake is set, it drops easily out of the tin with a sharp tap.

## TO MAKE THE HOLLY BISCUITS

1   Bake 16-18 holly biscuits (in a selection of sizes) using a holly-shape biscuit cutter following the instructions on page 199.
2   Divide 1 quantity of royal icing between 2 bowls and colour with 2 shades of green. Fit a piping bag with a No. 2 nozzle and 2 large tablespoons green icing. Repeat with another bag, nozzle and fill with other shade of green.
3   Thin the remaining green icings in the bowls with just enough water to achieve a runnier consistency. A spooned trail should settle on itself by the count of 10.
4   With each of the piping bags, hand pipe the outline of the cookies – using each colour for half the biscuits.
5   Fill a piping bag with one of the thinner, runnier icings and snip off the end. Flood half the cookies (with the contrasting outline). Smooth the icing into place with a clean, fine, damp paintbrush. Repeat with the other colour and the remaining biscuits.
6   Take the piping bags from before and over-pipe the outline of the biscuits and the central vein. Leave overnight until set.

These biscuits can be made up to 1 month in advance and stored in a clean white cake box or sealed plastic container lined with non-stick baking paper.

### TO MAKE THE POINSETTIA FLOWERS

1 Fit a piping bag with a No. 69 leaf nozzle and fill with the red royal icing (on the slightly stiff side). Line a board with non-stick baking paper and pipe the first 3 poinsettia leaves as a triangle to fit within a 6cm (2½-inch) diameter (you can draw a circle as a guide).

2 Pipe the next 3 leaves between the first to create a 6-petalled base flower. Repeat twice more so you have 3 separate flowers. Leave these to set for 30 minutes and then pipe a smaller set of 6 red petals inside the base layer as shown.

3 Leave them to set for 30 minutes and then hand pipe a series of small yellow pearls in the centre of the poinsettias using a No. 1.5 nozzle. These flowers are quite thick and may take up to 2 days to completely dry out to allow you to carefully lift them off the waxed paper with a small knife or crank handled palette knife.

4 These can be lifted straight onto the holly wreath and fixed in position with royal icing. It's a good idea to make a few more than you may need – to cover any breakages!

### TO ASSEMBLE THE WREATH

1 Knead and roll out the chocolate fondant sugar paste on a work surface lightly dusted with icing sugar.

2 Cover the wreath (it's a good idea to first place the wreath on a sheet of non-stick baking paper on a workboard) with the rolled sugar paste.

3 Press the paste into position and then use a 5cm (2 inch) deep round cutter to remove the fondant from the inside of the wreath. Neaten and trim the edges.

4 Carefully transfer the wreath to a cake board or stand to decorate.

5 Place the holly biscuits on the top of the cake to create a flat wreath, using royal icing to fix them in place. Add more biscuits and the poinsettia to complete the design.

6 Finish by fixing small red candy pearls into position with royal icing.

This cake will keep for 2 weeks – and should be kept cool, but not necessarily chilled. The holly biscuits can be enjoyed from the top and the cake served in thin wedge slices

**TOP TIP**

The poinsettia flowers can be hand-piped directly onto round gingerbread biscuits, making them easier to handle.

# ICED GINGERBREAD BISCUITS

*Christmas provides us all with the opportunity to showcase everyday bakes and showstopper cakes. From simple iced gingerbread biscuits to more elaborately decorated festive wreaths and gingerbread houses, these treats can be made up to four weeks in advance – to take you right through advent. Look out for Christmas cookie cutters on your travels. Alternatively, make your own templates from thick card and fashion the colours to complement your theme.*

**Makes about 30 biscuits**

*For the gingerbread biscuits*
425g (15oz) plain flour, plus extra for
    dusting
1 tbsp ground ginger
2 tsp ground cinnamon
½ tsp ground cloves
1 tsp ground nutmeg
1 tsp baking powder
½ tsp bicarbonate of soda
140g (4½oz) unsalted butter, softened
165g (5½oz) dark muscovado sugar
1 large egg yolk
165g (5½oz) treacle
1 tsp vanilla extract
1–2 tbsp milk

*For the royal icing*
3 large egg whites (about 125g/4oz)
500–600g (1lb 1oz–1lb 5oz) icing sugar
3 tbsp lemon juice

**TOP TIP**

The amount of icing can be adjusted depending on whether you are hand piping simple lines and pearls or decorating more fully with coloured flooding icing. As a rule of thumb, for 1 batch of biscuits, I would make a batch of royal icing with 125g (4oz) egg white and 500–600g (1lb 2oz–1lb 5oz) icing sugar. Double this if you are intending to flood in different colours.

## TO MAKE THE GINGERBREAD BISCUITS

1   In a mixing bowl, sift the flour, spices and raising agents together.
2   Cream the butter and sugar together in a separate large bowl.
3   Blend the egg yolk together with the black treacle, vanilla extract and milk. Whisk into the creamed mixture.
4   Add the flour to the batter and mix until the dough just comes together. Wrap the dough in cling film and chill for 30 minutes to rest.
5   Preheat the oven to 180°C fan (200°C/400°F/Gas 6) and line a baking sheet with non-stick baking paper.
6   Lightly knead the dough and roll out on a lightly floured work surface. Stamp out cookie shapes and place on the prepared baking sheet, spaced apart.
7   Bake for 8 minutes until golden. Transfer to a wire rack to cool.

## TO MAKE THE ROYAL ICING

1   Lightly whisk the egg white in a large, clean bowl until frothy.
2   Add the icing sugar and beat until the icing resembles freshly whipped double cream. Add the lemon juice through a tea strainer and continue beating until smooth and glossy. The icing should be mallowy and not too stiff. Aim for the consistency of freshly whipped double cream. If it looks grainy, add a little more egg white or cool water.

## TO DECORATE THE BISCUITS

1   To decorate, fit a piping bag with a No. 2 nozzle and fill with the white royal icing. Decorate the biscuits and then leave until set before storing in an airtight container.

Store at an airtight container at room temperature for up to a week.

# GINGERBREAD WREATH

*Take your Christmas creativity to a new level with this gingerbread wreath.
It makes a wonderful festive decoration and a perfect handmade, edible Christmas
gift that can be decorated up to a month in advance. Place on a cake board and
present in a cake box finished with festive ribbon. You could even leave a whole
wreath out for Santa, all his elves and the reindeer!*

**Makes 1 x 25cm (10 inch) wreath**

1 quantity of Iced Gingerbread Biscuits
    dough (see page 199)
1 quantity of Royal Icing (see page 199)
food colouring gels in colours of your
    choice

**TO MAKE THE BISCUITS**

1   Preheat the oven to 180°C fan (200°C/400°F/Gas 6).
2   Roll out half the biscuit dough onto a sheet of baking paper on
    a baking tray. Cut around a 25cm (10-inch) cake board with a
    15cm (6-inch) cake board inside to create the wreath.
3   Bake for 10–12 minutes until baked and the edges are turning
    brown. Remove from the oven and leave on the baking tray for
    2 minutes to cool and firm before transferring to a wire rack to
    cool completely.
4   Make 20 biscuits of different sizes and shapes with the remaining
    dough to decorate the wreath.

**TO DECORATE THE WREATH**

1   Decorate the biscuits with coloured royal icing. To flood, pipe
    the outline with royal icing and then thin the royal icing with
    a little water. Fill a piping bag with the thinner icing and flood
    inside the piped line. Use a fine paintbrush to move the icing to
    the corners. I've used this technique to decorate the bauble, star
    and holly leaves.
2   Leave the biscuits to firm and set for 2–3 hours before fixing
    into position on the wreath using royal icing – piled high and
    looking bountiful!

Store at an ambient temperature for up to 1 month. The biscuits
should be kept in an airtight tin or tub to retain freshness.

# GINGERBREAD HOUSES

*There is something nostalgic and sweet about gingerbread houses, for me, they epitomise Christmas. For the everyday project I have created a simple dwelling, complete with forest firs that can be displayed on a white iced cake board or stand – simple, charming and serene in the snowy iced winter wonderland.*

**Makes 3 x gingerbread houses and trees**

*For the gingerbread houses*
1 quantity of Iced Gingerbread Biscuits dough (see page 199)
1 quantity of Royal Icing (see page 199)
flour, for dusting
red and green food colouring gels

**TO MAKE THE GINGERBREAD HOUSES**

1   Preheat the oven to 180°C fan (200°C/400°F/Gas 6).
2   Roll the dough out on a lightly floured surface and carefully cut out the templates on pages 214-5. You will have 6 pieces for each house and 2–3 trees. From one batch of dough you should be able to make 3 gingerbread houses and trees. Use a rotary cutter (such as a pizza wheel) to carefully cut out the shapes – this prevents the dough from pulling. Alternatively, a small, sharp knife will work as well.
3   Place the shapes on a baking tray and bake for 8 minutes. Leave to cool on a wire rack before construction.

**TO ASSEMBLE THE GINGERBREAD HOUSES**

1   On a board, lay the back of the house face down and pipe two vertical lines of the white royal icing on the lower half just inside the edge and fix the two walls, perpendicular to the back. Repeat with the front of the house and fix this in position so you have the back, walls and front all in position, resting on its back and making sure the walls are straight and all pieces are in line with the foundations of the house.
2   Leave to set for 15 minutes or so, then carefully stand the house upright.
3   Pipe royal icing on the inside edge of the 2 roof pieces and fix these simultaneously in position over the house. Gently squeeze together so the roof is even. Leave until set.
4   Lay the house on its back again to pipe the front. With a No. 2 piping nozzle and coloured royal icing, hand pipe the windows, door and wreath decoration before standing up and hand piping the detail on the roof. Fit a piping bag with a star nozzle and fill with white royal icing and pipe a decorative join down the length of the roof. Leave until set. Now pipe alternating scallops and white snowy icicles over the front.
5   Pipe the trees as shown. Line a cake board or stand with white royal icing and set the scene with the house and fir trees.

**TOP TIP**

Each gingerbread house is made up of: 2 x roof panels, 2 x side panels, 1 x front and 1 x back.

Store at an ambient temperature for up to 1 month. The biscuits should be kept in an airtight tin or tub to retain freshness.

# CHRISTMAS ALPINE VILLAGE

*The weather outside is frightful, but this alpine village is so delightful! I love the fact this Christmas showstopper combines the best of both worlds – two tiers of rich fruity Christmas cake made with brandy and decorated with gingerbread houses and white iced fir trees. Something for everyone! I have made a 15cm (6 inch) and 25cm (10 inch) round cake, which have been covered in marzipan and white fondant sugar paste and stacked centrally on a 34cm (14 inch) square cake board.*

**Serves 60**

*For the alpine village*

2 quantities of Rich Celebration Fruit
    Cake mixture (see page 207)

boiled apricot jam, for brushing

brandy, for brushing

2kg (4½lb) marzipan

icing sugar, for dusting

3kg (6½lb) white fondant sugar paste

1 assembled Gingerbread House
    (see page 203)

1 quantity of Iced Gingerbread Biscuit
    dough (see page 199)

2 quantities of Royal Icing (see page
    199), coloured red, white and green

6 dowling rods

## TOP TIP

Bake your favourite cake for the alpine village – it doesn't have to be fruit cake. This idea can be created on a single tier, which can make a lovely Christmas gift. Change the colours to complement your theme and overload with as many Hansel and Gretel sweets as you like!

## TO MAKE THE CAKES

1   Preheat the oven to 125–130°C fan (145–150°C/275–300°F/ Gas 1½).

2   Divide the fruit cake mixture between a 15cm (6 inch) and 25cm (10-inch) round, deep cake tin.

3   Bake the smaller cake for 2¾ hours and the larger cake for 3½ hours.

## TO ASSEMBLE THE ALPINE VILLAGE

1   Brush the cakes with the boiled apricot jam. Roll out the marzipan on a clean work surface dusted with icing sugar to a thickness of 4–5mm (⅛ inch) and cover the smaller cake. Trim the excess and add this to the remaining marzipan to repeat and cover the larger tier.

2   Knead and roll out the white fondant sugar paste and use it to cover the cake board, brushed first with a little cool water. Trim with a sharp knife. Brush the cakes with brandy. Knead and roll out half the remaining fondant sugar paste on a clean work surface lightly dusted with icing sugar to a thickness of 4–5mm (⅛ inch) and cover the smaller cake. Trim the excess and add this to the remaining fondant sugar paste to repeat and cover the larger tier.

3   Leave to firm overnight and then stack the tiers centrally with internal dowelling rods trimmed to the height of the base tier for support on the base board. Fix in position with white royal icing.

4   Fix a length of grosgrain ribbon around the base board using a glue stick and around the base of each tier fixed with royal icing.

5   Make one gingerbread house as before and leave until set before fixing in position on the top tier.

6   Make the front of 14 other different shaped houses using the biscuit design (I used 3 variations in total) and 12 trees – 6 large, 6 small.

7   Decorate the village with red, white and green colours and leave to set. Fix the houses in position with white royal icing and then position the fir trees in front of the houses as shown. Leave until set. Let it snow! Let it snow! Let it snow!

# SIMPLE CELEBRATION FRUIT CAKE

*This simple fruit celebration cake is just that! It is so moist, rich, fruity and gently spiced. It does not have the dry cake crumb and burnt fruit you may associate with other fruit cakes you have tasted. The vine fruits are first washed and then soaked in brandy and orange liqueur for up to a week before baking. The cake is made by melting the butter with the dark caramelised sugars, giving it a wonderfully moist, dense texture.*

**Makes 1 x 20cm (8 inch) square cake**

*For the cake*

400g (14oz) naturally coloured glacé cherries

300g (11oz) sultanas

500g (1lb 2oz) seedless raisins

500g (1lb 2oz) currants

40g (1½oz) chopped stem ginger

150ml (5fl oz) brandy

50ml (2fl oz) orange liqueur

250g (9oz) unsalted butter

250g (9oz) dark muscovado sugar

1 tbsp treacle

4–5 large eggs, beaten (weigh the eggs to ensure you have the same weight as the butter, sugar and flour: 250g/9oz)

250g (9oz) plain flour

½ tsp baking powder

2 tsp ground cinnamon

2 tsp ground ginger

2 tsp ground nutmeg

½ tsp ground cloves

2 tsp mixed spice

*For the decoration*

3 tbsp apricot jam

4 tbsp brandy

350g (12oz) selection of dried fruit and nuts of your choice

## TO MAKE THE CAKE

1 Measure all the fruits into a large bowl and wash thoroughly with cold water until it runs clear. Drain the fruit through a metal sieve and tip into a fresh large bowl.

2 Add the chopped ginger and pour over the brandy and orange liqueur. Cover and leave it to infuse at room temperature for at least 48 hours (or up to a week).

3 When you are ready to make the cake, preheat the oven to 125-130°C fan (140–150°C/275–300°F/Gas 1–2) and line the base and sides of a 20cm (8-inch) square tin.

4 Place the butter and sugar in a large heavy-based saucepan and heat until melted. Stir in the treacle. Remove from the heat and leave to cool.

5 Slowly add the eggs to the melted liquid and stir until fully mixed.

6 In a separate bowl, sift together the flour with the baking powder and the spices. Stir the flour into the liquid until smooth.

7 Pour the batter over the soaked fruit and stir with a wooden spoon until fully combined. The batter should be quite loose at this stage.

8 Transfer the batter to the tin and bake for 3¼ hours. A knife inserted in the cake will come out moist but not wet when the cake is baked. Remove the cake from the oven and place on a wire rack. Leave to cool in the tin before turning out. Peel away the baking paper and wrap in a fresh double layer of baking paper, followed by aluminium foil and store in a cool, dry place away from sunlight to mature for at least 4 weeks.

## TO DECORATE THE CAKE

1 Blend the apricot jam with the brandy in a small saucepan. Bring to the boil and stirring with a hand balloon whisk to create a smooth glaze.

2 Generously brush the surface of the cake with the glaze and arrange the nuts and dried fruits over the surface. Brush the remaining glaze over the surface.

This cake will keep at room temperature in a sealed container for up to 3 months.

# TEDDY BEAR CELEBRATION FRUIT CAKE

*A simple iced fruit cake can be adapted to suit any and every special occasion. From weddings to anniversaries, Christmas to christenings – the rich fruit cake stands up well to a celebratory Champagne toast and really does take centre stage. Guaranteed to impress with its fruity flavour, it can be decorated a million different ways for all of your showstoppers.*

**Makes 1 x 20cm (8 inch) square cake**

*For the cake*
1 x Rich Fruit Celebration Cake
    (see page 207)

*For the decoration*
3 tbsp apricot jam, boiled
1kg (2¼lb) marzipan
icing sugar, for dusting
brandy, for brushing
1kg (2¼lb) fondant sugar paste
1 quantity of Royal Icing (see page 199)
length of ribbon to surround the cake

*For the teddy bear*
400g (14oz) chocolate fondant
    sugar paste

**TO DECORATE THE CAKE**

1   Brush the top and sides of the cake with the boiled apricot jam.
2   Knead and roll the marzipan on a work surface lightly dusted with icing sugar to a thickness of about 3-5mm (⅛ inch). Lift over the cake and then shape and trim to neaten. Brush the cake with brandy.
3   Knead and roll the white fondant sugar paste on a work surface lightly dusted with icing sugar to a thickness of about 3-5mm (⅛ inch). Lift over the cake and then shape and trim to neaten. Leave to set before decorating, ideally overnight.
4   Fill a piping bag with the royal icing and a No. 2 or 3 nozzle. Mark points on the top edge of the cake and hand pipe garlands and bows all around the edge.
5   Fix a length of ribbon around the base of the cake and hold in position with royal icing.

### TO MAKE THE CHRISTMAS TEDDY BEAR

1  Start by rolling some chocolate fondant sugar paste into an egg shape for the body and a smaller ball shape for the head. Insert a cocktail stick in the body before fixing the head in position.
2  Roll 2 squat sausages of paste, cut each in half and use to shape and fix first the legs and then the arms in position. Mark the paws and claws with modelling tools or a sharp knife.
3  Shape 2 small beads of paste for the ears and fix these into position with a cone tool. Flatten a piece of paste for the muzzle and add the nose, eyes and detail.
4  Accessorise your bear with a Christmas hat and giant candy cane also fashioned from coloured fondant sugar paste. Leave these to dry before fixing into position with a little cooled water.
5  Leave the finished bear to firm before transferring to the cake.

This cake improves with keeping and although it can be made fresh, it benefits from at least 4 weeks maturing before serving. It will happily keep for up to 9 months stored in a cake tin once covered and decorated.

### TO MAKE A CHRISTENING BEAR

The teddy bear is a flexible and universally loved decoration that can be altered to decorate other celebration cakes. A baby bear makes the perfect christening cake decoration, simply fashion a bow and matching teddy bear from the fondant of your choice. Insert tiny lengths of dried spaghetti to hold the teddy bear's arms and legs in position and at an angle. Fiddly – but be patient. These can all be made well in advance and kept in an airtight container for up to 3 months or longer.

### TO MAKE A BIRTHDAY BEAR

To transform the teddy into a birthday bear, simply make a party hat and gift in the same colours. Insert a small length of cocktail stick into the gift to fix into the bear's body to hold it in position. Change the ribbon around the cake to compliment it.

CELEBRATION CAKES

# TEMPLATES

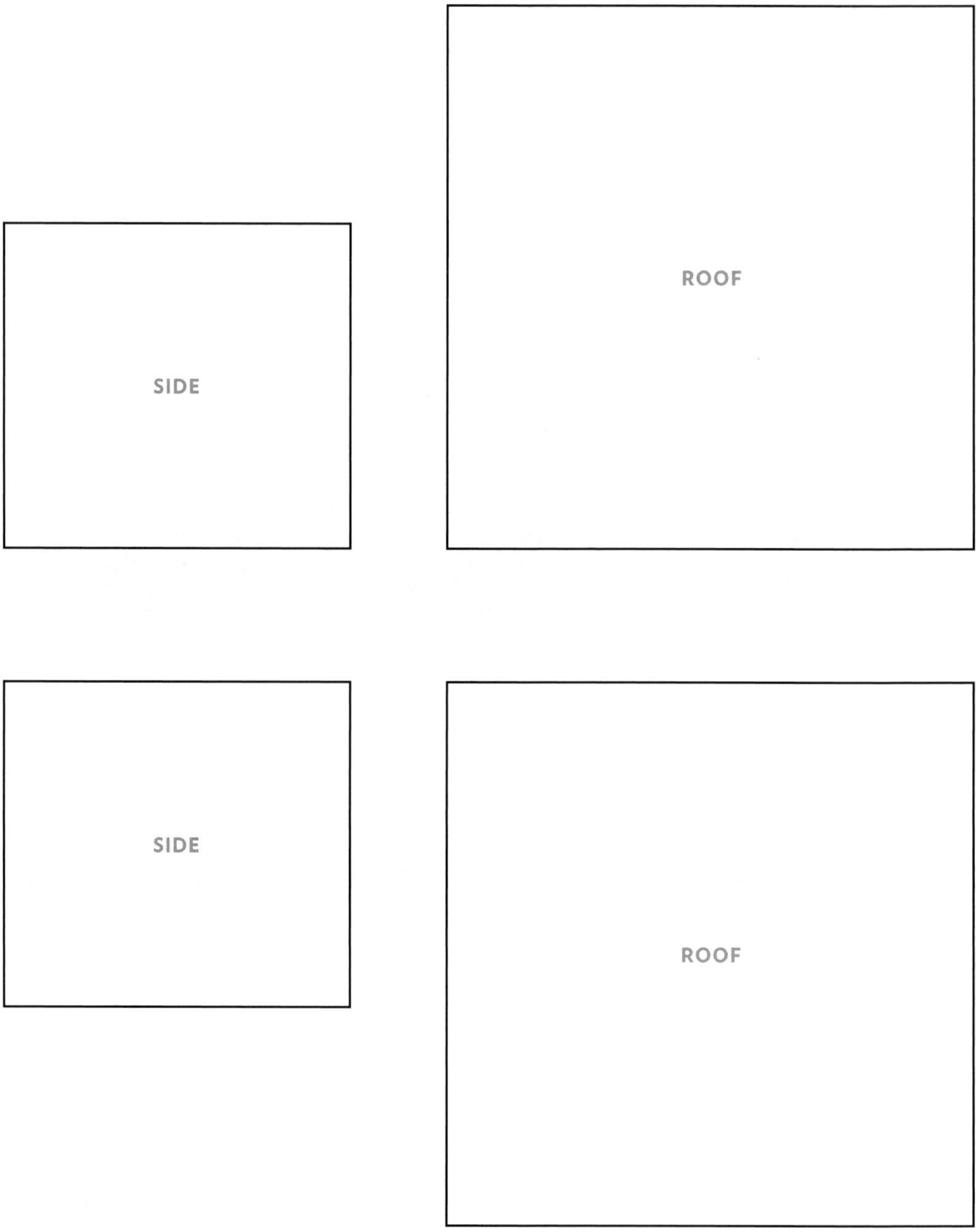

SIDE

ROOF

SIDE

ROOF

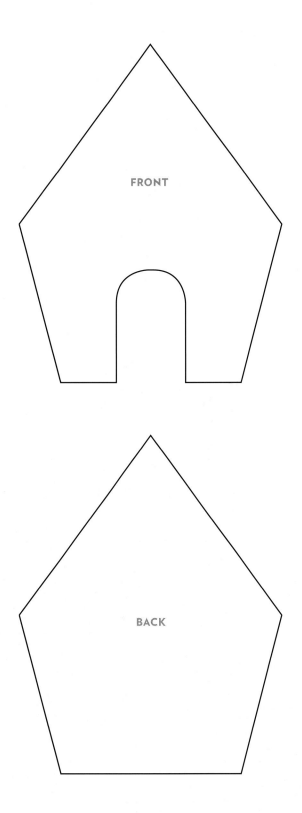

FRONT

BACK

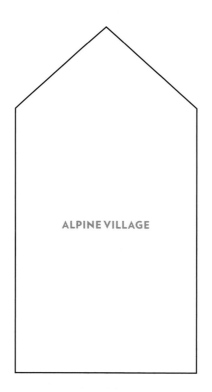

ALPINE VILLAGE

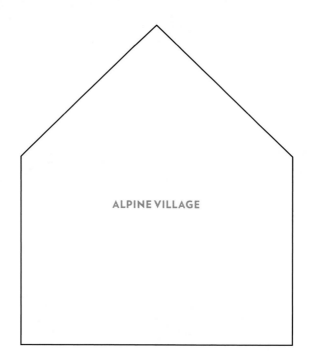

ALPINE VILLAGE

# INDEX

# ACKNOWLEDGEMENTS

As a cake designer it is a privilege to have the opportunity to work on a new book. It doesn't happen overnight and it doesn't happen single handedly! There are many people to thank – first and foremost my family – Phil, Marlow and George who always make me smile – and often laugh – especially at my own jokes! I love you all very much.

My enormous thanks goes to the team at Quarto who have supported me with this title. To Jessica and the newly arrived Oliver George born shortly after the final photo shoot – a baby brother for Sophia. It has always been a pleasure working with you – and a real treat with you in your new role for this book.

Cerys I love your energy and modern approach. Thank you for keeping the tone firmly on track and your support throughout the whole project. The first to celebrate a birthday with a cake from this book!

Lisa and Becci – I thank you both very much for being my dream team – photographer and stylist! It was such a treat to work with you both, your combined style, easy approach and ultimate professionalism made this book so enjoyable. You are such brilliantly talented ladies. I loved the fact you challenged my style. It was very refreshing. Not least of which, I feel like I lived Glastonbury! Thank you Lisa for the delicious bottle of wine at the end of the shoot – you star you!

Thank you to my talented Home Economist Emma – never marginal and always reliable. Thank you for supporting me throughout the project, putting up with me, encouraging me, second guessing me and always being on my wavelength! Especially as we were both enduring our elders' GCSE exam stress!

A special thank you to Marlow – for embracing your opportunity to assist Lisa with the photography on the shoot. Your personality, professionalism and helpful nature were much enjoyed and valued by us all. You were a wonderful addition to the shoot and contributed so much.

Thank you to Glenn and Charlotte – you have waved your wands, sprinkled your magic dust and brought all the mouthwatering projects to life in the book.

Thank you Allan Burns and all at Carr's flour for providing flour from your Scottish mill for these recipes – to my friends at SatinIce for the fondant sugar paste I used throughout the projects and to Maddocks Farm for the most gorgeous edible fresh flowers that literally filled the kitchen with fragrance and vibrancy.

Finally, a thank you to Lorraine and Carol at Black on Silver – as we embrace new and exciting opportunities in the world of cake – it is a pleasure to work with such experience and I can't wait for the next challenge!

First published in 2020 by
Frances Lincoln Publishing,
an imprint of The Quarto Group.
The Old Brewery, 6 Blundell Street
London, N7 9BH,
United Kingdom
T (0)20 7700 6700
www.QuartoKnows.com

A catalogue record for this book is available from the British Library.

ISBN  978 0 71124 707 9
Ebook ISBN  978 0 71124 708 6

10 9 8 7 6 5 4 3 2

Commissioning editors: Cerys Hughes and Melissa Hookway
Editor: Charlotte Frost
Food stylist: Rebecca Woods
Photographer: Lisa Linder
Photographer's assistant: Marlow Turner
Publisher: Jessica Axe

Thank you to Jane Sarre (janesarre.co.uk) for generously
providing the ceramics that appear on pages 41, 42 and 152.

Printed in Slovenia

Brimming with creative inspiration, how-to projects and useful information
to enrich your everyday life, Quarto Knows is a favourite destination for those
pursuing their interests and passions. Visit our site and dig deeper with our
books into your area of interest: Quarto Creates, Quarto Cooks, Quarto Homes,
Quarto Lives, Quarto Drives, Quarto Explores, Quarto Gifts, or Quarto Kids.